BEING THE GAFFER!

The Crazy World of the Football Manager

PRION

CONTENTS

FOREWORD BY
HARRY REDKNAPP

It's probably about time that football managers were given the credit they deserve and a book celebrating all of the famous and colourful characters to have ever graced the touchline on a freezing Saturday in February is a great starting point.

My word, times have changed since I reported to my first gaffer way back when. It was the great Ron Greenwood who was in charge at Upton Park when I first came through the ranks and incredibly, by the standards of today, he was still in charge seven years later when I left! Mind you, he had led the Hammers to their greatest triumphs, winning the FA Cup and European Cup-Winners' Cup.

He was an intelligent, thoughtful chap, who preached simplicity but also instilled the need for attacking enterprise among his players. He helped develop a lot of young talent and the likes of myself, Geoff Hurst and Trevor Brooking have a lot to thank him for.

Dear Ron cared about the game, as do all of the managers featured in the book, as you will read though with mixed results.

The game of football has changed a hell of a lot and so has the role of being a football manager. The pressures are so much more intense. Who can blame a manager for getting a little 'over excited' if the referee has just allowed an offside goal, which is likely to mean his team's fifth defeat on the bounce which is in turn going to mean the supporters chanting for him to be sacked, or possibly worse still, have the board offering you their full support!

Who'd be a football manager? I would every time!

INTRODUCTION

The original plan for this book was not to find the greatest managers of all time, although undoubtedly a high percentage of them are featured here. As such, this is not a definitive list of the world's most successful gaffers, which is open to too much subjectivity and bias. We were primarily attracted by managers who were interesting. Their inclusion was not reliant on silverware – they had to be flamboyant, controversial, infamous, quirky or different. For example, there is no doubt that Franz Beckenbauer or Johan Cruyff were better players and more successful managers than Dave Bassett or David Pleat. However, a string of relegations or a dramatic fall from grace can be every bit as memorable as a glorious cup campaign.

There were several themes which emerged in the writing process. For one, the best footballers rarely make the best managers, although there are some exceptions. A high number of top grade gaffers hailed from coal mining families, where it can be assumed they acquired the camaraderie, discipline and willpower to reach the pinnacle of their profession. Many of the greats used their war experiences to full effect in the dug-out. Notable others shone because they came to management early – either because their career never got started, or it was cut short through injury. And interestingly, only one in here was a goalkeeper!

Within this book, you will find the full spectrum of football manager: the shouters and screamers; the jokers and buffoons; the front page scandal merchants; and the intellectuals, who have thought their way to the top of the pile.

The book was a huge amount of fun to write and compile, so I hope you will enjoy reading it.

Ian Valentine, 2010

P.s. If any of the managers have been fired or hired since publication, then please accept our apologies. There's no such thing as job security for a football manager!

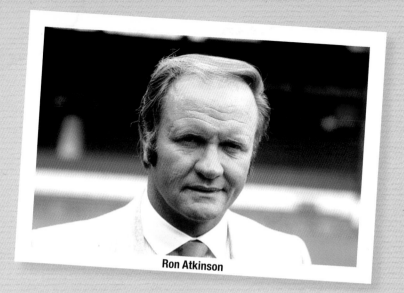

Ron Atkinson

Brian Clough

Malcolm Allison

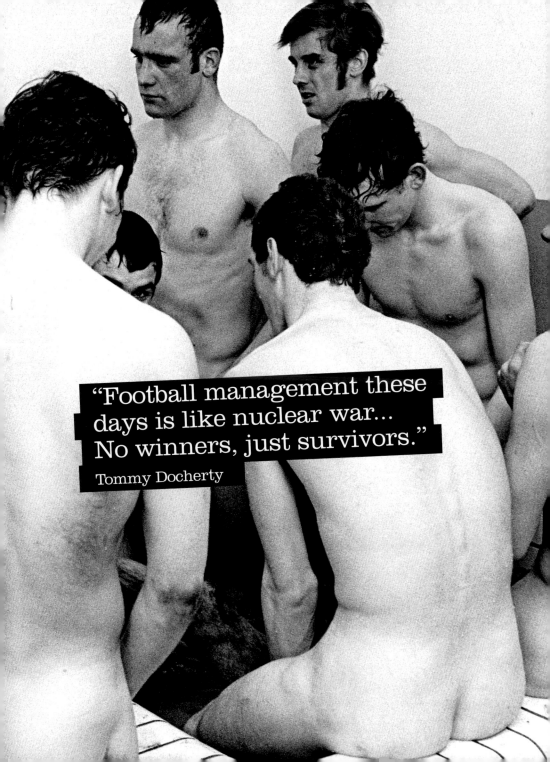

"Football management these days is like nuclear war... No winners, just survivors."

Tommy Docherty

MALCOLM ALLISON 'BIG MAL'

> "A lot of hard work went into this defeat." Malcolm Allison

Malcolm Allison was one of the most flamboyant characters of the sport who set the bar on sartorial elegance, which many others have attempted to emulate. Instantly recognizable in his sheepskin jacket and ostentatious fedora hat, with a fat cigar puffing beneath its wide rim, Allison was the original champagne-swigging playboy manager.

Allison was one of the many managers whose footballing career was cut short by ill-fortune: in his case a bout of tuberculosis which demanded the removal of a lung. Not that one lung ever curbed his desire to smoke. His first big break came in the 1960s as coach of Manchester City, under Joe Mercer, and Allison is widely credited for being the mastermind of the club's huge success over the following decade, arguably the most successful in their history.

His reputation as a showman was already secure by the time he took over at Crystal Palace in 1973. Having been relegated from the top flight that year, Palace were in need of inspiration, but Allison failed to become their messiah, as they dropped further, to the Third Division, in his first season. "Big cigar, big hat, big mouth" was how one fan described him, as Palace were receiving all the wrong press attention. However, in 1976, Allison came good, leading his team on an FA Cup charge to the semi-final. The media loved him, indulging his desire for

Malcolm Allison (1927–)
Nationality: English.
Managerial honours: One English League Championship, one FA Cup, one League Cup, one European Cup Winners' Cup (with Manchester City); one Portuguese League Championship, one Portuguese Cup (with Sporting Lisbon).

> **"John Bond has blackened my name with his insinuations about the private lives of football managers. Both my wives are upset."**
>
> Malcolm Allison

the spotlight, including a public affair with soft porn star Fiona Richmond, whom he coaxed into the club baths as his players soaked in their post-match glory.

Allison's sexploits would have provided a stream of front-page headlines for modern tabloids, but back then there was not the same kiss-and-tell culture. The flash beau even had a tryst with Christine Keeler, who would later bring down a Government minister. He adored the champagne and beautiful women lifestyle and wasn't afraid to flaunt it. Sven-Goran Eriksson had nothing on Big Mal.

As with so many of his colleagues, Allison struggled between genius and goat. There were the moments of triumph, especially at Manchester City and later Sporting Lisbon, but there were also gambling debts, booze binges, prison cells and acrimonious fall-outs. "You're not a real manager unless you've been sacked" said Allison, who was definitely a real manager. Yet for all his peaks and troughs, he did set a standard for other showmen to follow and we should all be grateful for that.

BRIAN 'CLOUGHIE' CLOUGH

> "We talked about it for 20 minutes and then we decided I was right."
>
> Brian Clough

Eccentric, hot-headed, witty and determined, 'Cloughie' had that X-factor, which allowed him to conjure up results that more conventional managers could only envy. Bringing Derby County from relative obscurity to European prominence could be written off as good fortune. That he repeated it with Nottingham Forest confirmed the man's genius.

Born in Middlesbrough, the young Clough set a record for post-war marksmanship, netting 251 goals in just 274 matches for both Middlesbrough and Sunderland. A knee injury cut him down in his prime, but he soon found a calling as a manager. It says much about his impact on Derby County that there were demonstrations on the streets when he was pushed out by the chairman. Not only had he lifted the Rams from the Second Division to win the top flight title, but he had blazed a trail to the semi-final of the European Cup, falling eventually to Italian giants Juventus. Clough always maintained that the tie was fixed by a bribed referee, describing the Italians as "cheating bastards."

Their loss was Nottingham Forest's gain, as for the next 18 years, Clough led the club to unprecedented success. Forest were regularly at the top of the league, having won it in 1978, the year after promotion back to the First Division. But it was the back-to-back European Cup wins in 1979 and 1980 that guaranteed Clough a place at the managerial top-table.

He was never far from the next controversy, quick to shoot a verbal arrow at anyone who stood in his way. Liverpool legend Bill Shankly captured Clough's ability to talk his way

Brian Clough (1935–2004)
Nationality: English.
Managerial honours:
One English League Championship, European Cup semi-finalist (with Derby County); one English League Championship, two European Cups, four League Cups, one European Super Cup (with Nottingham Forest).

THE BIG MATCH

"I wouldn't say I was the best manager in the business. But I was in the top one." Brian Clough

"If God had wanted us to play football in the clouds, he'd have put grass up there."

Brian Clough

into your heart or under your skin. "He's worse than the rain in Manchester, but at least God stops the rain in Manchester occasionally." But when a journalist complained that Clough was outspoken, Shankly replied, "Laddie, that man scored 200 goals in 270 matches – an incredible record – and he has won cup after cup as a manager. When he talks, pin back your ears."

Clough's forthright manner was a winner on the terraces, but it didn't half put the back up of the establishment. He is often described as the best manager England never had, but when asked his thoughts on the matter, the reply was typical Clough. "They thought I was going to change (the FA) lock, stock and barrel. They were shrewd because that's exactly what I would have done."

He had a simple formula for winning matches: keep hold of the ball and it was always his way or the M1 motorway. "We talk about it for 20 minutes and then we decide I was right."

Despite the ups and downs, he was sent to the stands for the second half of the season for striking a Forest supporter that ran on the pitch and he was implicated in the 'bungs' scandal of the early Nineties, Clough was always respected by the fans as a gentleman who demanded the highest standards from his players and who could bring the best from his team. He spoke their language. "I want no epitaphs of profound history and all that type of thing. I contributed – I would hope they would say that, and I would hope somebody liked me." Indeed, he made Nottingham Forest a household name across the globe. "I wouldn't say I was the best manager in the business. But I was in the top one." For many, that still rings true.

BILL 'SHANKS' SHANKLY

> "A football team is like a piano. You need eight men to carry it and three who can play the damn thing." Bill Shankly

Born just before the Great War in the tough mining village of Glenbuck in Ayrshire, Shankly was schooled in the escapist power of football. As a skilled midfielder, the sport was his ticket away from the toil and danger of the coal mines, so when he eventually arrived at Anfield in 1959, Shankly was determined that the Saturday afternoon match should be a chance for the fans to forget the drudgery of working life.

For Shankly, the club belonged to the fans. The players were allowed no airs and graces either and certainly not the same pampering as modern stars. When tough defender Tommy Smith tried to explain to his manager that his bandaged knee was injured, Shankly replied: "Take that poof bandage off. And what do you mean about YOUR knee? It's Liverpool's knee!"

Shanks thought like a fan on the Anfield terraces, which meant having a pop at their rivals across the Mersey, Everton, who were also a leading force in English football at the time. Not that Shankly would give them the credit for that publicly. At the funeral of Everton legend Dixie Dean, Shankly was able to raise a smile at his old rival's expense. "I know this is a sad occasion but I think that Dixie would be amazed to know that

Bill Shankly: 1913–1981
Nationality: Scottish
Managerial honours:
Three English League
Championships, two
FA Cups, one UEFA
Cup (with Liverpool).

"Just go out and drop a few hand grenades all over the place son." Bill Shankly to Kevin Keegan

"Take that poof bandage off. And what do you mean about YOUR knee? It's Liverpool's knee!" Bill Shankly

even in death he could draw a bigger crowd than Everton can on a Saturday afternoon."

As a manager, he was fortunate to have a backroom staff of Bob Paisley and Joe Fagan, but it was his drive and charisma that hauled a proud team from the doldrums back to their rightful place. Way back in his Glenbuck days, he had been taught the benefit of 5-a-side football training, with close, one-touch passing; and his players would practice these drills until it was second nature. This free-flowing style would become the envy of the European game. Perhaps his crowning moment came in the 1974 FA Cup Final at Wembley when his team terrorised Newcastle United 3:0 with such speed and skill that the score line flattered the runners-up.

That summer, Shankly retired unexpectedly. Although his successor Paisley would take the club onto greater glory, it was Shanks who had laid the foundations. When he died suddenly in 1981, the fans showed their undying respect, unfurling a banner at the Kop End that read 'Shankly Lives Forever.' Before his death, Shankly had a chance to sum up his relationship with the supporters. "I felt that the Liverpool people were my kind of people," he said, "I never cheated them and they never let me down."

SIR ALEX 'FERGIE' FERGUSON

> "When a player is at his peak, he feels he can climb Mount Everest in his slippers." Sir Alex Ferguson

Dour, red-nosed and provocative Fergie may be, but he has also filled the trophy cabinet and coffers of Manchester United for the last two decades with a brand of attacking football that commands a global audience.

As a player, it did not really happen for the Glasgow-born player. He often struggled to make the first team, flitting from club to club, before arriving at his beloved Glasgow Rangers. However, he was scapegoated for conceding a goal in the 1969 Scottish Cup final. Therefore, it was as a 32-year-old that Ferguson took to management, learning the ropes at East Stirlingshire and St Mirren. Even at that early stage, he was gaining a name for being a disciplinarian, as one of his strikers said: "I've never been afraid of anyone before, but Ferguson was a frightening bastard from the start." When he arrived at Aberdeen, it took a few seasons to gain the respect of the older players, who nicknamed him Furious Fergie. But when the team won the League in 1980, the first time a non-Old Firm team had taken the title in 15 years, the Pittodrie masses took their manager to heart.

Two more league titles would follow, as well as regular success in the domestic cup. But it was the European success in 1983, which had the Aberdonians dancing in the streets. Defeating both Bayern Munich and mighty Real Madrid, Fergie

Sir Alex Ferguson (1941–)
Nationality: Scottish.
Managerial honours: Three Scottish League Championships, four Scottish Cups, one Scottish League Cup, one European Cup Winners Cup, one UEFA Super Cup (with Aberdeen FC); eleven English League Championships, five FA Cups, four League Cups, two UEFA Champions League, one UEFA Cup Winners Cup, one Intercontinental Cup, one UEFA Super Cup (with Manchester United). Managed Scotland.

> **"When an Italian says it's pasta, I check under the sauce to make sure. They are innovators of the smokescreen."** Sir Alex Ferguson

brought the Cup Winners' Cup to the east coast of Scotland.

A brief spell as temporary Scotland manager, following the sudden death of his great mentor Jock Stein, propelled Ferguson into the hot seat of Old Trafford. He has since added 19 more trophies, including an unprecedented ten League titles (with three on the bounce), five FA Cups and winning the UEFA Champions League in 1999 meant he bagged a remarkable treble. Following Solskjaer's last gasp winner against Bayern Munich to win the European Cup, Ferguson is known to have exclaimed "Football eh? Bloody hell." This year's dramatic penalty shoot-out against Chelsea to win the Champions' League, completing the double over the West London side, proved that Fergie retains that Midas touch on the biggest stage.

Ferguson has never been backward in coming forward, reveling in any scrap with an opposition manager and defending his players in the face of criticism.

His mantra has long been that no player is bigger than the club, shown by his achievement at outlasting first-rate stars such as Jaap Stam and David Beckham, who left with plenty to offer the club. The hairdryer reprimands, teacup throwing and boot kicking during the half-time interval are stuff of legend, while Ferguson's obsessive control of his players, allegedly dragging a few out of nightclubs, has doubtless annoyed some, but helped others.

There have been disappointments – indeed any season without the league title is deemed as such – but it is highly unlikely that another manager, British or otherwise, will come close to his list of achievements.

BOB PAISLEY

> "If you're not sure what to do with the ball, just pop it in the net and we'll discuss your options afterwards." Bob Paisley

Bob Paisley was a big man with a huge heart, who masterminded Liverpool's dominance over the rest of the domestic and European club scene throughout the 70s and early 80s. It is sometimes said that Paisley benefited from the hard work put in by Bill Shankly in rebuilding the club's reputation, but that is to forget the role played by Paisley throughout Shankly's reign as team physio and assistant coach. Paisley's list of achievements would be greater still, if we were to add the three league titles, two FA Cups and UEFA Cup won as a member of the Boot Room in the 15 years under Shankly.

Having made 252 post-war appearances for Liverpool, Paisley could lay claim to being an Anfield legend before he entered coaching. On retiring, the gentle giant from Durham taught himself the skills of physiotherapy, a role usually filled by an ex-player in the days before professional masseurs, dieticians and faith healers. Paisley quickly won a reputation for being able to diagnose and fix injuries, which he added to his natural ability to read a game.

Paisley was yet another successful manager with a mining background and his upbringing at Hetton-le-Hole in County Durham taught him a work ethic and modesty that would serve him well. His father was badly injured in the mines and his brother died of scarlet fever whilst Paisley was fighting in Italy. The story goes that he was so shaken by the news that he walked about in a daze, inadvertently dodging a

Bob Paisley (1919–1996)
Nationality: English.
Managerial honours: Six English League Championships,
three European Cups, European Super Cup, UEFA Cup,
three League Cup (with Liverpool).

> ## "Mind you, I've been here during the bad times too – one year we came second." Bob Paisley

shell with his name on it. If you are looking for glitzy tabloid scandals, champagne or dancing girls, then Paisley is a disappointment. There were no outspoken comments or risky politics. One tribute to him described him as "the genius in a flat cap, the sporting icon in a pair of carpet slippers, the world renowned physiotherapist in a woolly cardigan." But he could be ruthless with his players when he had to be, drawing from his own disappointment at being dropped for an FA Cup final.

His first job as manager was to ensure a smooth progression from one era to the next, after Shankly shocked the Kop by standing down in 1974. Uncle Bob initially struggled, leading to the comment, "Mind you, I've been here during the bad times too – one year we came second." The next year, his team topped the league and the cups never stopped coming, including a unique trio of European titles. While he inherited a squad of fine players, Paisley could be shrewd in the transfer market, replacing Keegan with Dalglish to keep the good times rolling.

Paisley saw his beloved Liverpool lift 19 trophies in just nine years, a total surpassed by only Sir Alex Ferguson, who took twice the time. He was voted manager of the year on six out of the nine years. He did not have the dress style of Mourinho, the charisma of Busby or the fear factor of Fergie, but when it comes to churning out results, Paisley stands out alone amongst the best of the English managers.

Rinus Michels (1928–2005)
Nationality: Dutch.
Managerial honours: four Dutch League Championships, one
European Cup, three Dutch Cups (with Ajax); one Spanish League and
one Spanish Cup (with Barcelona); German Cup (Cologne); European
Championships winner and World Cup runner-up (Holland).

'THE GENERAL' RINUS MICHEL

> ## "Professional football is something like war. Whoever behaves too properly, is lost." Rinus Michel

Dutch wizard Rinus Michels is credited with developing the most admired style of play available to the modern manager: total football. While other successful gaffers have won trophies and built dynasties using long ball tactics or the *catenaccio* counter-attack model so favoured by the Italians, Michels chose to create a team that could attack from any area of the pitch with players who could shine in any position.

'The General' was fortunate that the triple-European Cup winning Ajax and Dutch team in the late 60s and early 70s boasted the remarkable talents of Johan Cruyff, who was so technically gifted that he could have held down a place in any position. The rest of the squad were no slouches either and would adapt to fill in the gaps, so that there was always a man in space who could do what was necessary. The final of the 1974 World Cup, in which the Dutch won a penalty from the kick-off having passed the ball round the Germans 13 times, was perhaps the pinnacle of Michel's *totaalvoetbal*.

The key to its success was discipline. Known as 'The Sphinx' in his homeland, he was also a fearsome intellect who used to insist on reading a whole book on every foreign match trip. After a successful stint with Barcelona, he took the reins again of Holland and inspired them to their only major championship win, Euro 88. Again, he was blessed with such stars as Marco Van Basten, Ruud Gullit and Frank Rijkaard at his disposal. In 1999 'The General' was named coach of the century by FIFA.

HELENIO HERRERA 'THE WIZARD'

> "We won without getting off the bus." Helenio Herrera

Helenio Herrera was quite simply one of the most successful managers of his or any other generation. Herrera, who won 16 major trophies, including two European Cups, was a renowned tactician whose strategy earned him praise and criticism in equal measure. His negative style of play, built on a stubborn defence that aimed to win 1-0, was evidently successful, but it earned him more trophies than friends.

The *catenaccio* (padlock) system during the glory years at Inter Milan, involved playing five at the back. Although there was license for the wingbacks to counter-attack, the emphasis was on defending a lead rather than extending it.

Herrera is also famed for inventing the mind-games that are so common nowadays. He would often boast his team had won the game even before they left the dressing room, predicting the scoreline with arrogant assumption. He would encourage his players to meditate before games and as they gathered in the changing room, he would hurl balls at them, screaming in their faces, before embracing each and every one. There were motivational slogans posted around the Inter dressing room, with proclamations such as "who doesn't give it all, gives nothing" and the Three Musketeers' "all for one and one for all." Creating the right image was everything. One player was suspended for telling the press "we came to play in Rome" instead of 'we came to win in Rome.'

Yet for all that Herrera has become infamous for, the man was a winner with a record few others can match.

Helenio Herrera
(1910–1997)
Nationality:
Argentinian/French.
Managerial honours:
Two Spanish League Championships (with Atletico Madrid); two Spanish League Championships, two Spanish Cups, two Fairs Cup (with Barcelona); three Italian League Championships, two European Cups, two Intercontinental Cup (with Inter Milan); one Italian Cup (with Roma). Managed Spain and Italy

JOCK WALLACE

Jock Wallace, one of the very few goalkeepers to progress into a successful career as a manager, worked in the coal mines and fought as a commando in the Malayan jungle. As such, he was tough as six inch nails.

Recognition first came in 1967, when, as player-manager of Berwick Rangers, he overturned Glasgow Rangers in what was probably the greatest ever Scottish Cup upset. If you can beat them, join them too, and in 1970 he was signed as coach at Ibrox under Willie Waddell. Two years later, Rangers won the European Cup Winners' Cup. Wallace then ended the nine consecutive Celtic league wins in 1975 – an achievement he is still adored for on one side of the city – before snaring the Scottish Treble twice.

Wallace insisted that his players were fitter than the opposition. In the off-season, he would hold sprint sessions on the punishing sand dunes south of Edinburgh. The chef Gordon Ramsay, who played as a pro for Rangers under Wallace, remembers him as a Scottish version of Mike Tyson. "When he wanted to rip your arse out, he would crucify you." Gary Lineker, who played under Wallace during the Scot's stint at Leicester City, was frightened to death of the man. "He once pinned me against the dressing room wall at half-time and called me a lazy English this and that," he remembers. "We were 2-0 up and I'd scored both goals!"

Yet for all his ferocity, Wallace was a fair man who understood the fans. At the time, Rangers needed a manager who would never take a backward step and Wallace was that soldier.

Jock Wallace (1935–1996)
Nationality: Scottish.
Managerial honours: Three Scottish League Championships, three Scottish League Cups, three Scottish Cups, one European Cup-Winner's Cup (with Glasgow Rangers).

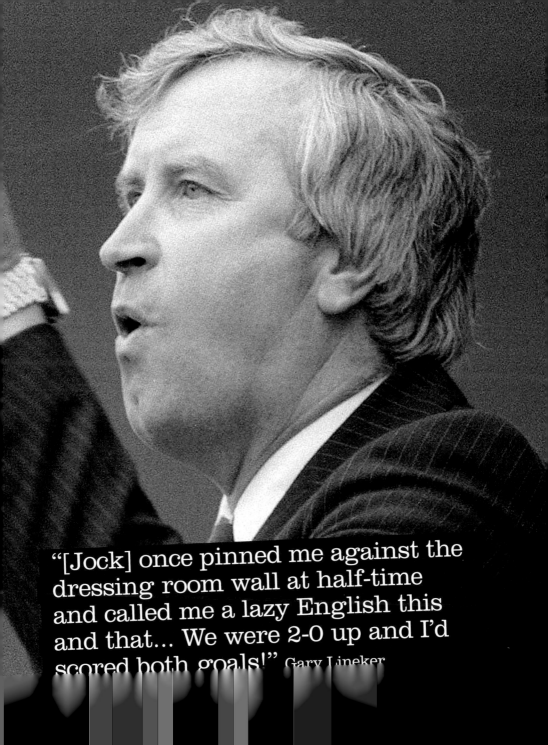

"[Jock] once pinned me against the dressing room wall at half-time and called me a lazy English this and that... We were 2-0 up and I'd scored both goals!" Gary Lineker

DON REVIE

> "Keep your hair short, your clothes smart and don't get caught up with loose girls."
> Don Revie

Don Revie was loved and loathed in equal measure. For the Leeds United faithful, he was a talismanic manager who elevated the Yorkshire club from mediocrity to become one of the most consistent, attractive and feared teams in Europe. For the critics, of which there were many, Revie encouraged foul play on the pitch and engaged in foul play off it, culminating in accusations of bribery and personal greed.

From the mid 1960s to the mid 1970s, Revie's Leeds were feared as being a tough, even violent, opposition. Revie, who as a skilful midfielder himself knew what it was like to get a good kicking, did eventually deliver a more aesthetic playing style, but it is for their aggressive defence that the 'Giants' were infamous.

Winning was everything for Revie, no matter the cost, and he made sure his team bought into his mindset. He had quirky superstitions, such as wearing the same suit until the team lost. Then there was the gypsy woman summoned to exorcise the curse that Revie believed was bringing bad luck to Elland Road. He was a meticulous planner, gathering minute details on the opposition and running drills until his players' heads swam. Above all, he instilled a discipline and work ethic in his team, on and off the pitch, which produced results. Even the hardest of his troops could be cut to the quick by a Revie stare or snarl.

Don Revie (1927–1989)
Nationality: English.
Managerial honours:
Two English League Championships, one FA Cup, one League Cup, two Inter-Cities Fairs Cups (with Leeds United). Managed England and United Arab Emirates.

> "When he [Eddie Gray] plays on snow, he doesn't leave any footprints." Don Revie

Eventually, England came calling, but his will to mould footballers to his own ideas of perfection meant that his stint as manager in the mid-Seventies was doomed to failure. His Leeds players could tolerate his cantankerous nit-picking, but the stars from other clubs would not. He left under a cloud in 1977 to become manager of the UAE, amid media accusations of greed, and even treason.

Rumours circulated that Revie had been involved in bribery and match-fixing in his early years as a manager, in particular from Sunderland manager Bob Stokoe, whose team stunned Leeds in 1973 to win the FA Cup final. He was also said to have tried to influence the result against Wolves in 1972 in order to win the championship, earning the nickname "Don Readies". Leeds lost the match and came second in the league. The allegations were never proven, and Revie was successful in bringing legal action against detractors in the media, but the mud stuck.

In 1987, Revie was diagnosed with motor neurone disease and he died two years later. While the Leeds supporters never lost faith with him throughout his retirement, it took a while for the rest of the country to forgive.

ALLY MacLEOD

> ## "I think Ally believes tactics are a new kind of peppermint."
> ### Anonymous Scottish defender on Ally MacLeod

"My name is Ally MacLeod and I am a winner," said the Scotland coach when he met his new squad before the qualifiers for the 1978 World Cup in Argentina. Indeed, MacLeod did win enough games to qualify for the finals, but it is as a heroic loser that the manager will long be remembered.

"We'll be back with at least a medal" was the next confident boast before the team left for South America, with the delirious fans singing "We're on the march with Ally's Army," a song that reached Number 6 in the UK charts when remixed by Andy Cameron. England had not qualified, so Scotland would carry the Home Nations' hopes abroad. 25,000 Scots came to cheer the squad at Hampden before they left. "What do you plan to do after Scotland win the World Cup?" asked one journalist. "Retain it," replied MacLeod.

But Scotland performed like amateurs in their first two matches: a loss to Peru and a draw with lowly Iran. In typical infuriating fashion, the team then played one of the greatest games in their nation's history, beating the eventual finalists Holland, 3-2, including Archie Gemmill's wonder goal. Scotland were eliminated on goal difference and MacLeod did not last much longer as manager.

Unbowed, MacLeod later consoled himself that he was "a very good manager who just happened to have a few disastrous days, once upon a time, in Argentina." He was a tragic hero, but a lasting reminder that building expectation is a risky business.

Ally MacLeod (1931–2004)
Nationality: Scottish.
Managerial honours:
One Scottish League Cup (with Aberdeen).
Managed Scotland.

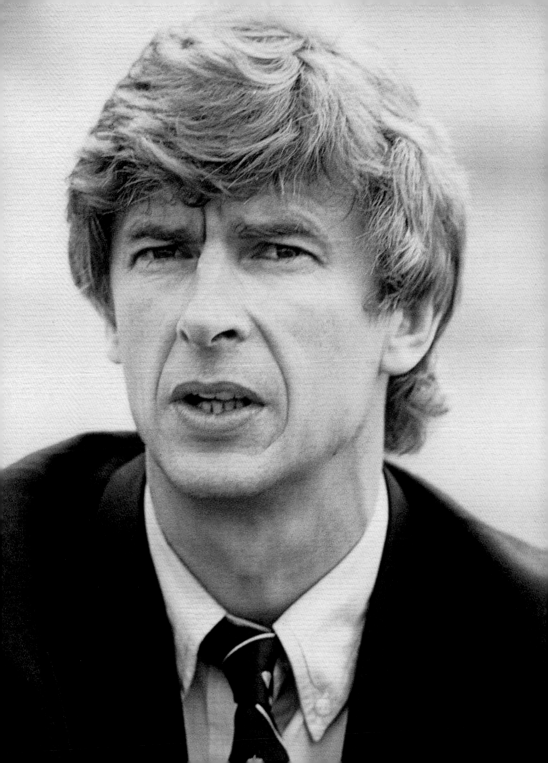

ARSENE WENGER 'THE PROFESSOR'

"I didn't see the incident."
Arsene Wenger

Arsene Wenger is the pin-up for those who like a thinking manager. Almost geeky in appearance with his round glasses, Wenger has become the most successful of all the foreign managers to coach in the British Isles, developing a brand of attacking football at Arsenal which is the envy of many.

His own playing career never took flight, but while many of his contemporaries won silverware, Wenger was honing the most important weapon in his arsenal: his brain. A masters degree in economics followed a degree in engineering, as the young man from Strasbourg exercised his grey cells. However, at Monaco, he soon proved that this intellect was coupled with instinct, as he uncovered the first in a long line of hidden gems, signing players such as George Weah and Youri Djorkaeff.

A move to Japan taught him the benefits of a simple, robust diet and a personal fitness ethic that has been credited with prolonging several players under his care. Indeed, the famous flat back four of Arsenal, which had been playing throughout the Nineties, were given a second wind when he arrived at Highbury, as was the genius of Dennis Bergkamp.

A double of league championship and FA Cup in his second season at Arsenal cemented his place at the club, while the arrival of French stars Thierry Henry, Robert Pires and Sylvain Wiltord, all bought with the profit he made from the sale of Nicolas Anelka, took the team to new levels. Henry, especially,

Arsene Wenger (1949–)
Nationality: French.
Managerial honours:
One French League Championship, one French Cup (with Monaco); one Japanese Super Cup, one Emperor's Cup (with Nagoya Grampus Eight); three English League Championships, four FA Cups, European Cup runner-up (with Arsenal).

> "When you're dealing with someone who only has a pair of underpants on, if you take his underpants off, he has nothing left – he's naked. You're better off trying to find him a pair of trousers to complement him rather than change him." Arsene Wenger

matured under Wenger's watchful eye, to lay a claim to being the best on the planet.

The Frenchman has relished the rivalry with Manchester United and latterly Chelsea, ever eager to stoke the cauldron. It has bubbled over at times, most notably during 'pizzagate' in 2004, when Sir Alex Ferguson's side ended the remarkable 49 game unbeaten streak at Old Trafford. Players were said to have thrown food at each other in the dug-out, followed by accusations by Wenger that striker Ruud Van Nistelroy was a cheat.

Whilst manager of Chelsea, Jose Mourinho came to verbal blows with Wenger, labelling the Frenchman a 'voyeur' and claiming he was obsessed by the rival London club. Success often breeds contempt from the envious and Wenger's Arsenal have been accused of being dirty and violent in the past, borne out with a high level of red cards. Wenger has been quick to defend his players, saying with a shrug that, "I did not see it" or that his team are victimised by referees. He also fielded the first team with no home-grown players, attracting further criticism by pundits. But for Wenger, it is about putting the most exciting 11 on the pitch at any one time. "When you represent a club it's about values and qualities, not about passports."

Week in, week out, Arsenal play the most attractive football in the league, yet their supporters are growing impatient for silverware.

DAVE 'HARRY' BASSETT

> ## "I honestly believe we can go all the way to Wembley, unless somebody knocks us out."
> Dave Bassett

Londoner Dave Bassett was a man for a crisis. Whenever a team was looking a lost cause, Bassett would be called upon to lead them to safety. Sometimes it worked: indeed he can boast the highest number of league promotions of any manager, with seven under his belt. But there were also five seasons when he managed a team that was relegated, including two in one season.

His own playing career never quite took off, but as a young manager, he soon piloted non-league Wimbledon's passage through the divisions to the top flight in just five years, between 1981 and 1986, including a quarter-final of the FA Cup. It was truly an astonishing accomplishment, although the so-called Crazy Gang won no fans outside Plough Lane for their 'route-one' long ball tactics, enforced by physical tackles by the likes of Hollywood hardman Vinny Jones. Although Bassett had since left, the Wimbledon FA Cup win in 1988 against Liverpool must still rate as one of the greatest upsets ever.

While the Crazy Gang ran riot at Wembley, Bassett oversaw the relegation of first Watford and then Sheffield United, although he did then gain back-to-back promotions with the Blades. The fans showed their appreciation by stripping him down to his underpants. That was how it was with Bassett: he was either scrapping at the top or bottom of the table.

Dave Bassett (1944–)
Nationality: English.
Managerial honours:
English Division Two League Championship (with Nottingham Forest); Division Four League Championship (with Wimbledon).

FABIO CAPELLO

"I just can't stand ankle socks. When a gentleman crosses his legs and the trouser leg rides up to show hairy shins at the top of the sock it offends my eyes."

Fabio Capello

It is easy to see why the Football Association were so keen to get Fabio Capello to coach England: wherever he has managed, silverware has been won. Indeed, he guided all four clubs to their league title at least once. In the case of AC Milan, Capello oversaw a period of extended success, including four Scudetto in five years, a whole season undefeated in 1991, and the demolition of Barcelona 4-0 to win the European Cup in 1994. His team of 'Invincibles' were also runners-up twice, despite the name.

Himself a gifted and robust midfielder, who scored the only goal in Italy's win over England at Wembley in 1973, Capello has a reputation for favouring a defensive gameplan, but that is possibly misleading. He has shown great pragmatism over his career, unleashing the creative skills of his AC Milan team, but subduing the under-achieving Galacticos of Real Madrid to play a conservative brand of football. Both styles won the league.

By banning golf and insisting that the players dine together, he quickly trimmed back the matey-matey fluff endorsed by Steve McClaren. This ability to stand up to egos has already brought the best from Team England, orchestrating its smooth passage into the 2010 FIFA World Cup. He could well be the difference between success and failure in the latter stages.

Fabio Capello (1946–)
Nationality: Italian.
Managerial honours: Four Italian League Championships, one European Cup (with AC Milan); two Spanish League Championships (with Real Madrid); one Italian League Championship (with Roma); two Italian League Championships (with Juventus – later rescinded). Managed England.

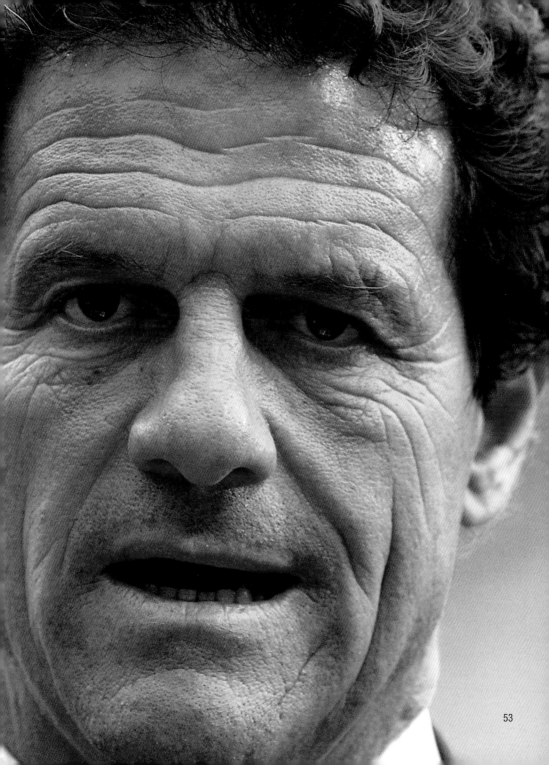

Carlos Bilardo (1939–)
Nationality: Argentinian.
Managerial honours:
One Argentinian League Championship
(with Estudiantes); one World Cup,
World Cup runner-up (with Argentina).

CARLOS BILARDO

"If you look at how many [World Cup] Finals have been played, how many people have reached them and how many are still alive, you realise there aren't many at all."

Carlos Bilardo

There are some footballers with brains and many without. Argentina's 1986 World Cup winning manager Carlos Bilardo certainly falls into the first category. Even as a player, he was valued for his tactical nous, leading a team of young firebrands called the "killer juveniles" as midfield anchor. Their victory over Sir Matt Busby's Manchester United in the 1968 Intercontinental Cup was hailed as the flowering of Argentinian club football.

Perhaps there was no better man therefore to harness the natural genius of Diego Maradona during the Eighties, as Argentina vied with West Germany for world domination. There were troughs among his peaks, notably as coach of Colombia, when he was fired for failing to qualify for the 1982 World Cup. He courted controversy by taking the role as manager of Libya (where many of the players, including President Gaddafi's son, were trained by shamed sprinter Ben Johnson). Bilardo also caused consternation when snapped swigging from a champagne bottle during a final spell at Estudiantes. He claimed it was filled with Gatorade, but the mud stuck.

Aside from being a thoughtful manager, teacher and skilled commentator, *El Narigon* (big nose) is also a qualified physician, specialising in rectal cancer and gynaecology. He has recently been critical of modern football, saying it is governed by money and one-dimensional players, rather than the passion and skill of his youth.

CARLO ANCELOTTI

"We can say we have the cake and now we're just missing the cherry on top. Carlo Ancelotti

Lesser managers might have baulked at the prospect of confronting the egos at Chelsea Football Club. But AC Milan's Carlo Ancelotti lifted trophies as a player alongside the likes of Marco Van Basten, Ruud Gullit and Franco Baresi. He won the Champions League as a manager with star-names such as Andriy Shevchenko, Kaka and Paolo Maldini. He survived the eccentricities of Silvio Berlusconi as club president, as well as an Italian match-fixing scandal. Stamford Bridge had little to faze one of only six men to win the European Cup as a player and manager.

Despite being an integral part of the attacking Rossoneri (red/blacks) team in the late 80s, Carletto the coach has been accused of being over-defensive in his tactics. But any manager with the riches of Maldini, Alessandro Nesta, Cafu, Jaap Stam and John Terry at the back can be forgiven for sitting on a lead.

Understandably, Meelan's failure to defend three-nil at half time to Rafael Benitez' Liverpool in Istanbul remains a haunting memory for Ancelotti, despite beating the same opposition in the final two years later. "They were six minutes of black-out," he wrote in his autobiography, giving an insight into the helplessness of managers when their team implodes. "We were a perfect machine in total breakdown. It couldn't be happening. I was paralysed with no time to react. Who would have managed to stay lucid in those circumstances?"

In the dug-out, Ancelotti has the cool exterior of a hired gun, complete with dark suit and scowl. But this born achiever, who has a penchant for cured pork and cigarettes, enjoys a reputation for creating team unity and a happy dressing room. He has the players' respect and trust. It is little wonder that he has already brought success to west London.

Carlo Ancelotti (1959-)
Nationality: Italian
Player honours: Four Italian League Championships, four Italian Cups (with Roma); two Italian League Championships, two European Cups (with AC Milan); 26 caps (1 goal) for Italy.
Managerial honours: Intertoto Cup (with Juventus); one Italian League Championship, one Italian Cup, two European Cup (with AC Milan); one FA Community Shield (with Chelsea).

HARRY CATTERICK

"Let's have this skillful football..." Harry Catterick

The name Harry Catterick ought to be mentioned more often in the same breath as his contemporaries Shankly, Busby and Revie, for his achievement in taking Everton to the very top of the English pile was every bit as impressive. But he was no extrovert, preferring to brood in the shadows.

Catterick was not renowned as a tracksuit-wearing dervish on the training ground, but rather an authoritarian who was quick to identify a problem and sort it. His players talked about his ability to recognise a weakness and put it right at half time. The strategy was a throw-back to the Evertonian 'School of Science' of their early days, when the Toffees played expansive, attractive football. While the first league title in 1963 was built on a rock-solid defence, the second in 1970 was all about attacking flair, inspired by the 'Holy Trinity' of Alan Ball, Howard Kendall and Colin Harvey. Their ability to pass rings round the hard men of Leeds United was a defining moment in Catterick's era.

Whilst ruling the club with an iron clipboard, Catterick was fiercely protective of his players, who respected him entirely. He could take risks too, including a decision to pick the inexperienced Mike Trebilcock as striker in the 1966 FA Cup final. Trebilcock scored two as Everton fought back from two goals down to win 3-2. He was so unknown that the BBC commentator Kenneth Wolstenholme called him 'Trebilco' for the entire match.

Catterick's dream team was broken up in the early 1970s and the stress eventually sparked a heart attack. He died 10 years later of the same affliction, having watched his beloved Everton win an FA Cup match at Goodison.

Harry Catterick (1919–1985)
Nationality: English.
Managerial honours: Two English League Championships, one FA Cup (with Everton).

DAVID PLEAT

> "I was inbred into this game by my father."
>
> David Pleat

David Pleat falls into the category of managers who are famous for their extra-curricular activities rather than silverware in the cabinet. Yet another gaffer whose playing career was cut short by injury, Pleat did enjoy a successful start to his management career, inspiring Luton Town to reach the English top flight, where they stayed for 10 years. With his star burning brightly, Pleat was invited to take charge of Tottenham Hotspur, where he immediately led them to third in the division and a cup run to the FA Cup final.

The surprise defeat to Coventry City at Wembley signalled a reverse in fortune. Soon, there were rumours circulating that Pleat had been arrested for kerb-crawling. Spurs dispensed with his services when it became apparent he had been convicted for the offence on three separate occasions, giving rise to the joke that Pleat drove the slowest car in London.

Pleat returned to management, but with only sporadic success, unable to snare any trophies. However, he has enjoyed a media career as a pundit for *The Guardian* newspaper, ITV and BBC Radio, handing down pearls of wisdom such as "I was inbred into the game by my father"; "this is a real cat and carrot situation"; and "I've seen some players with very big feet, and some with very small feet." A true one-off.

David Pleat (1945–)
Nationality: English.
Managerial honours: One FA Cup Final (with Tottenham Hotspur).

FRANK WATT

"The Newcastle team of the 1900's would give any modern side a two goal start and beat them, and further more, beat them at a trot." Peter McWilliam

Frank Watt combined a love of football and business to take Newcastle United to the top of the domestic game within just 10 years of the club's creation. Between 1895 and 1930, Watt acted as club secretary, although he was manager in all but name, picking the team and buying new players. As a Scotsman, he was just one of many Jocks who made the trip south and under his guidance the Magpies won four league titles and the FA Cup twice in six attempts, including a sequence of five FA Cup finals in seven years. Only Sir Alex Ferguson has taken an English team to the FA Cup final more times.

Watt's first task was in uniting the city, which had previously been divided into Newcastle East End and Newcastle West End. East End used to offer their players 15 shillings for a win and ten bob for a draw or defeat, as well as a bonus of one shilling a man per goal, so it was perhaps no surprise that the club was built on attacking foundations. Even in its infancy, the Toon Army expected their team to play flowing, expansive, exciting football, no matter if it meant putting the win in jeopardy. It is a habit they have never quite been able to shake off.

Yet Frank was one manager who won more than he lost, tossing the Geordies the juiciest of bones, which they are so desperate to chew on again.

Frank Watt (–1932)
Nationality: Scottish.
Managerial honours:
Four English League Championships, two FA Cups (with Newcastle United).

SVEN-GORAN ERIKSSON

> ## "We don't want front pages, we want back pages."
> Sven-Goran Eriksson

When you think of Sven-Goran Eriksson, what springs to mind first? It could be the image of a quiet, pensive man in glasses, searching for the winning formula, or the clever headlines of the redtops as they revealed another sex allegation? For some, he is the master tactician who delivered silverware for a host of European teams, the professor who led England to a 5-1 win over Germany, or the comeback kid who tried turn round the fortunes of proud clubs such as Manchester City and Notts County. Others are not so generous: there were the cries of anguish as England butchered three opportunities to advance at major championships, or the enormous pots of cash paid by the FA for precious little gain.

For all of the more tawdry baggage that the press seem determined to saddle Sven, he has been an extremely successful manager, shadowed all the way by his henchman Tord Grip. No other manager has achieved a cup and league double in three different countries (Sweden, Portugal and Italy), while he did lead Lazio to their greatest run of silverware. He delivered the necessary qualification to the World Cup (twice) and Euro Finals with England, taking them to the quarter-finals each time. Their elimination to Brazil and Portugal (twice on penalties) was far from entirely his fault.

In another era, Sven's private life would have remained exactly that. Besides, the alleged affair with TV presenter Ulrika Jonsson and tantrums by long-term partner Nancy Dell'Olio probably enhanced his reputation among football fans rather than the opposite. Yet, for all the ups and downs, it is surely the Swede who has come out on top.

Sven-Goran Eriksson (1948–)
Nationality: Swedish.
Managerial honours: Two Swedish Cups, two Swedish League Championships, one UEFA Cup (with Gothenburg); three Portuguese League Championships, one Portuguese Cup, European Cup Runners-up (with Benfica); one Italian Cup (with Roma); one Italian Cup (with Sampdoria); one Italian Cup, one UEFA Cup Winners' Cup, one UEFA Super Cup, one Italian League Championship (with Lazio). Managed England, Mexico and Cote d'Ivoire.

HERBERT CHAPMAN

> **"It works. I am just waiting until everybody has copied it, then I shall come up with something new."**
>
> Herbert Chapman on his famous 'M' formation.

No other manager has left a more lasting impression on the British game than Arsenal's Herbert Chapman. His innovations in the late Twenties and early Thirties were years ahead of his contemporaries, dragging a tired, predictable sport by its bootlaces into the modern era. Add to that his achievement in taking Huddersfield to their first major honours and propelling his North London club to heights which they still enjoy today and we have one of the most important managers in the history of British football. Indeed, the *Sunday Times* in 2004 declared him to be the greatest of them all.

Another manager with a coal mining background, Chapman showed a remarkably cultured and thoughtful attitude to football, rather than the fire and brimstone strategy adopted by many of his peers. For example, he took an active role in the aesthetics of the club, redesigning the strip to include white sleeves and hooped socks, so the team could recognize each other more easily. He insisted that the flowers in the Director's Lounge were in the opposition's colours as a mark of respect. He told the players to clap all four sides of the stadium to say thank you to the fans, as well as introducing the first white balls instead of the old drab brown so that the spectators could better see the ball in play. He is even credited for persuading London Transport to rename Gillespie Road tube station to the 'Arsenal' tube station. Tinkering further,

Herbert Chapman (1878–1934)
Nationality: English.
Managerial honours:
One FA Cup, two English League Championships (with Huddersfield Town); one FA Cup, two English League Championships (with Arsenal).

> ## "I would borrow one [idea] from a programme boy at Highbury, if it were a good one."
> Herbert Chapman

he dropped the 'The' from Arsenal, so that the club would be alphabetically top of the league.

Chapman was the first to put numbers on players' backs, he put clocks in Highbury Stadium to tell spectators how long there was left, he provided physiotherapists for his players, and he championed electronic turnstiles, synthetic pitches and floodlights in response to the threat of speedway and greyhound racing. He would try any idea to modernise the game, saying once "I would borrow one from a programme boy at Highbury, if it were a good one." Perhaps his greatest achievement, however, was wrestling the team selection decisions away from the boardroom; a success that every manager since has to thank him for.

Herbert Chapman also recognised the need for feeder clubs, which again are the norm today. In 1931 he effectively took over Clapton Orient, later known as Leyton Orient, where he could give his juniors a run-out against genuine opposition. This dedication to grassroots proved to be his ultimate undoing, as he insisted on watching an Arsenal Thirds team play on a wet January evening in 1934, against medical advice. Within a week he had died of pneumonia, at the age of 55.

Many of the big names in this book took clubs from the doldrums to greatness and Chapman did that with both Huddersfield and Arsenal. Yet, it was for his legacy to every other club in the league that Chapman is most fondly remembered.

JOHN BECK

> **"I only said four words and three of them were 'You were useless'."** John Beck

If you were to make a list of the world's greatest managers, then Cambridge United's John Beck would not feature in the first one thousand. But when it comes to picking the most bizarre governors in the history of the sport, then Beck demands inclusion on the top table. Beck could be described as innovative and crafty, a master of gamesmanship. But that is to miss the point. He was obsessed by winning and would employ whatever devious means in his power to surmount the odds. If the end justifies the means, then he was a success. Between 1990 and 1992, Cambridge United were promoted twice to reach fifth in the old Second Division, where they were knocked out in the semi-final of the Premiership play-offs. Beck also led his men to back-to-back sixth rounds in the FA Cup, a remarkable achievement for so lowly a side.

But this was not a fairy story built on sweat, guts and inspiration. Oh no. That would leave too much to chance. Whenever possible, Beck would attempt to gain a psychological edge over his opponents. He had a vast array of tricks in his locker from playing loud music in the opposition dressing room at half time and turning up their heaters, deflating their practice balls before the match, or getting the ball boys to roll the ball in the mud before opposition throw-ins. He also moved the opposition manager's dug-out, so it was no longer on the half-way line. Yet, perhaps he is most

John Beck (1954–)
Nationality: English.
Managerial honours: Promoted Cambridge United from Fourth to Second Division in two years. Twice reached the sixth round of the FA Cup.

> **"Many of us thought Beck was mad, but he put a very good team together ... masters of simply battering the opposition into submission."**
> Dion Dublin

notorious for allegedly telling the apprentices to spike the away team's cups of tea at half time, replacing sugar with salt and even getting them to urinate in the tea pot.

His own players were not immune from his flights of fancy. Before matches, he would insist they took cold showers or throw buckets of ice cold water over themselves. During a fit of rage, he head-butted striker Steve Claridge, who duly punched him back. On the pitch, his long-ball tactics were vilified by the rest of the football league. Any throw in the oppo's half would be launched long into the penalty box by players trained in the art. To help his limited strategy, Beck used to insist that the groundsman leave the grass to grow long in the corners, often to six inches, so that the defenders would have to clear it into the stands. That would allow another long throw into the box, where the big lads were waiting.

When the results started to dry up, the club's patience quickly waned and Beck was sacked in 1993. Yet for the Cambridge faithful, there is still a place in their hearts for the enigmatic John Beck.

SIR BOBBY ROBSON

"We didn't underestimate them. They were a lot better than we thought." Sir Bobby Robson

Few of the managers in this book had such a full playing career as Sir Bobby Robson, yet another son of a miner, who played over 600 competitive matches for Fulham, West Brom and England. Early management proved tricky, but when he arrived at Ipswich Town, the worm turned. Over the next 13 years at Portman Road, he spent less than £1 million on transfers, but led the Tractor Boys to FA Cup and UEFA Cup victories.

England came calling and Robson took the England fans on a rollercoaster ride for almost the next decade. There were highs – he only lost one qualifying match in 28 – as well as reaching three major Championships. But there were lows too, such as the Maradona 'Hand of God' in 1986 and the penalty shoot-out loss to West Germany in 1990. "Not a day goes by when I do not think about the semi-final and other choices I might have made," he once wrote. However, he was soon back in the big time, leading PSV Eindhoven, FC Porto and Barcelona to success in a way precious few British managers have achieved abroad. Eventually, he was given the opportunity to coach his beloved Newcastle United, although he never quite brought the Magpies the glory they still crave.

Managing well beyond retirement age, Sir Bobby set the standard in longevity for others to follow. When he died in 2009, after a dignified fight with cancer, English and foreign football fans alike mourned his passing. "If you're a painter, you don't get rich until you're dead," he once commented. "The same happens with managers. You're never appreciated until you're gone, and then people say: 'Oh, he was OK'. Just like Picasso."

Sir Bobby Robson
(1933–2009)
Nationality: English.
Managerial honours: One FA Cup, one UEFA Cup (with Ipswich Town); one Dutch League Championship (with PSV Eindhoven); one Portuguese Cup, one Portuguese League Championship (with Porto); one Spanish Cup, one European Cup Winners' Cup (with Barcelona). Managed England.

VALERY LOBANOVSKY

"There is no such thing as a striker, a midfielder, a defender... only footballers." Valery Lobanovsky

When Valery Vasilyevich Lobanovsky died following a pitch-side stroke in 2002, there were 200,000 at his funeral, testament to the status he held in his hometown of Kiev. As a player, he helped bring success to the club in the old USSR, but as a manager he carved a path to become the dominant Soviet side and latterly one of the most potent forces in Europe.

Perhaps the brilliance of Lobanovsky lay in the fact he had a foot planted in both manager camps: he was a thinker and tactician in the Herrera or Mourinho mould, but also a passionate man of the people like Busby or Shankly. Even as far back as the Seventies, Lobanovsky was programming computers to detail players' abilities and weaknesses, a tool that drew suspicious glances from the KGB.

His gameplan was an extension of the Dutch 'Total Football' model. "I don't like players having positions," Lobanovsky once said. "There is no such thing as a striker, a midfielder, a defender. There are only footballers and they should be able to do everything on the pitch."

This was no easy format to pull off, but the results speak for themselves. The brooding giant launched the careers of several European stars during his time at Kiev, including Oleg Blokhin and Igor Belanov in the Eighties and Andrei Schevchenko (who he named 'The White Ronaldo') and Sergei Rebrov in the Nineties. It is perhaps a reflection of his ability to bring the best from a player that many of his protégés struggled to recreate the magic when they left his care.

Valery Lobanovsky
(1939–2002)
Nationality: Ukrainian.
Managerial honours:
Eight Soviet League Championships, six Soviet Cups, five Ukrainian League Championships, two European Cup Winners' Cup (with Dynamo Kiev). Olympic Bronze, European Championships runner-up (with USSR). Managed United Arab Emirates, Kuwait and Ukraine.

GLENN HODDLE

"If he was chocolate, Glenn Hoddle would eat himself."
Anonymous England player

Throughout his career, Hoddle left himself open to attack on account of his self-confidence, which was often interpreted as arrogance. The most gifted player of his generation, with vision and technical skill off both feet that shone in an era of long ball tactics, he was perhaps a decade ahead of his time.

Yet, the slings and arrows (he was nicknamed Glenda by opposition fans) bounced off his flowing mullet and he even had the inner strength to sing the dreadful Diamond Lights with Chris Waddle in 1987. By that stage, he had begun his controversial relationship with faith healer Eileen Drewery, who he would later employ as a member of the England back room staff.

As a manager, Hod often found it hard to gain the respect of his players, who felt they were being talked at like children. Wins were a result of his tactical brilliance, while losses were blamed on players' weaknesses. For example, he was perhaps too ready for red-carded David Beckham to shoulder the blame of England's loss to Argentina in the 1998 World Cup.

It was not his management style or record that ended his England career, however, but his views on disability and reincarnation: "You and I have been physically given two hands and two legs and half-decent brains. Some people have not been born like that for a reason. The karma is working from another lifetime. What you sow you reap." Following an appeal from Prime Minister Tony Blair on a daytime chat show, the FA asked him to step down. The players, who were angered that their coach had revealed the changing room secrets in a published diary, were not sad to see him go.

Glenn Hoddle (1957–)
Nationality: English.
Managerial honours:
One FA Cup (with Chelsea).
Managed England.

GRAEME SOUNESS

"Working with people on a field turns me on." Graeme Souness

Graeme Souness' combative style and bristling moustache as an attacking midfielder won him plaudits and medals galore, but as a manager his bull in a china shop approach could drive players, fans (especially opposition fans) and chairmen to distraction. His playing pedigree was beyond question, skippering Liverpool to the forefront of European football under Bob Paisley. He represented Scotland in three World Cups and was one of the few British players to have tasted success abroad, with Sampdoria.

But it was back at Rangers in Glasgow that he cut his teeth as a player-manager, reversing the decline of the Ibrox team in the 80s. But he was never far from controversy. For a start he signed several English stars and then Maurice Johnston, a Catholic, from under the noses of rivals Celtic. There were spats with the league which led to touch-line bans, only for Souness to name himself among the substitutes, so he could still patrol the dug-out.

From the successes at Rangers, Souness struggled at Liverpool, where he often warred with players and alienated the fans who had once adored him. Turkey followed, where the warrior Scot was welcomed by the partisan fans of Galatasaray. After an away cup match against arch rivals Fenerbahce, Souness all but started a stadium riot when he planted a huge Galatasaray flag in the middle of the home team's pitch.

Returning to Britain, Souness achieved immortality by signing bogus Senegal star Ali Dia for Southampton after his agent pretended to be George Weah on the phone. Dia, voted by The Times as the worst footballer ever, lasted just 20 minutes as a sub before being subbed himself.

Graeme Souness (1953–)
Nationality: Scottish.
Managerial honours: Four Scottish League Championships, four Scottish League Cups (with Rangers); one FA Cup (with Liverpool); one Turkish Cup, one Turkish Super Cup (with Galatasaray); one League Cup (with Blackburn Rovers).

GRAHAM TAYLOR

> "Being an ex-England manager, one that failed to qualify for the World Cup, is like being a dead politician." Graham Taylor

Graham Taylor belongs to the long list of English managers famous for who they were rather than what they achieved. Taylor's trophy cabinet has gathered dust throughout his playing and managing career, but he still managed to generate some of the best tabloid headlines in the history of sports journalism.

As a manager for Elton John's Watford team in the late Seventies and early Eighties, Taylor was a miracle maker. In five years, he hauled the Hornets from the Fourth Division to the First, where they even qualified for the UEFA Cup, having finished second in their first season of top flight football, although critics at the time pointed to his reliance on the long ball tactic.

His promotion to England came as a surprise in 1990 and it started poorly with a shambolic display in the 1992 European Championships. Trailing to Sweden, Taylor opted to substitute the captain Gary Lineker, who needed another goal to equal Bobby Charlton's national scoring record. It would be Lineker's last match as England were eliminated. *The Sun* revelled in a "Swedes 2-Turnips 1" headline portraying Taylor's bonce as the root vegetable. When they then lost to Spain en route to bungling qualification to the 1994 World Cup, he became a Spanish Onion.

Taylor was hounded from England to universal approval (there was even a 'Sack Taylor' candidate in a 1993 by-election) but he did bounce back to complete 1,000 matches as a league manager and still enjoys a voice in the media. But ask him to think of a vegetable and it probably won't be a carrot.

Graham Taylor (1944–)
Nationality: English.
Managerial honours:
FA Cup runners-up (with Watford); English League Championship runners-up (with Aston Villa). Managed England.

"It's a game we've got to win.
It's also a game we've not got to lose."

Graham Taylor

HARRY REDKNAPP

> **"You will never get the sack for having an untidy desk. You only get the sack if you lose games and buy bad players."** Harry Redknapp

Harry Redknapp enjoys a reputation as one of the best man-managers in the English top flight, whose shrewd signings have taken Portsmouth to the big time. Plain spoken and personable, often to his own downfall, Harry has perhaps won more friends than trophies over his 1,000 plus games in management, but there are indications that his best years may be ahead of him.

He cut his teeth as a gaffer at Bournemouth, which he led out of the Third Division for the first time in a century. Sticking close to his roots, Harry, father of footballer turned pundit Jamie, then took the reins at West Ham United, fostering the skills of current England players Frank Lampard (his nephew), Rio Ferdinand, Michael Carrick and Joe Cole. At the time, he was willing to inspect any new talent, including a spectator during a pre-season friendly against Oxford City. The fan, with 'West Ham' tattooed on his red neck, had been shouting abuse throughout the first half. Harry called his bluff and invited him to get changed at half time. "That's the great Bulgarian Tittyshev!" Harry told a journalist. Tittyshev duly scored in the second half.

West Ham reached fifth in the Premiership, before Harry was sacked for spilling too many beans about the club to a magazine. "I sat down with these guys from the fanzine and they started asking me questions and I spoke to them in the way I'd talk to someone in a pub. I said a few things I shouldn't

Harry Redknapp
(1947–)
Nationality: English.
Managerial honours:
One English Third Division Championship (with Bournemouth AFC); one Intertoto Cup (with West Ham United); one FA Cup, one English League Divsion Two Championship (with Portsmouth).

> **"With the foreign players it's more difficult. Most of them don't even bother with the golf, they don't want to go racing. They don't even drink."** Harry Redknapp

have said and walked into the chairman's office expecting to sign a contract and walked out without a job!"

It did allow him to start his relationship with Portsmouth, who he helped gain promotion to the Premier League. However, following a dispute with the chairman, Redknapp moved to nearby rivals Southampton, which earned him criticism from sections of Fratton Park but those detractors were won round as he returned to Portsmouth, saved them from relegation and then delivered a string of excellent results with his ability to find the best in players who were struggling at other clubs. A career highlight came in the FA Cup in the 2007/2008 season when Harry made it a hat-trick of shock wins over Manchester United, (he beat them with Bournemouth and West Ham), en route to Pompey lifting the cup at Wembley for the first time since 1939.

Harry was head hunted by Tottenham Hotspur early in the 2008-9 season, leading them out of the relegation zone to eighth in the table and reaching the final of the League Cup. The following season, following a handful of crafty signings, Tottenham eventually shook off their mid-table tag and began competing with the top four.

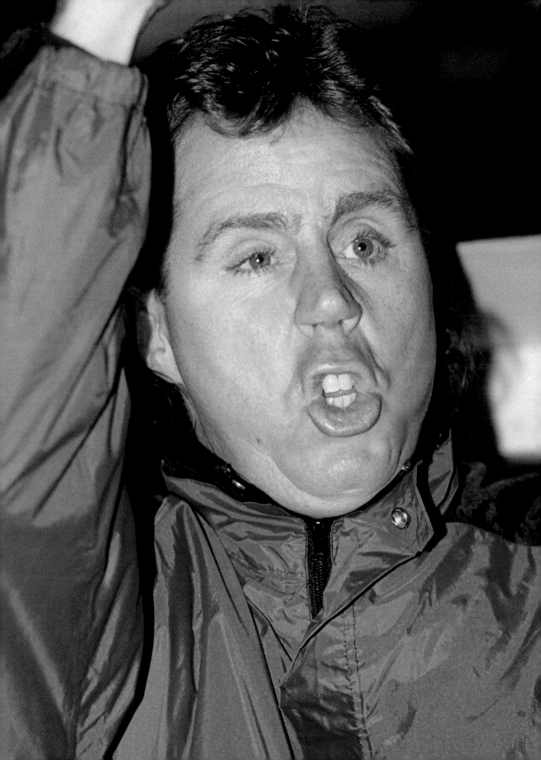

HOWARD KENDALL

"My own autobiography, which was written by Ian Ross...."

Howard Kendall

In 2008, Everton fans of Howard Kendall launched a petition to have their legend knighted. With just 547 co-signers, it looks unlikely that their ruse will work, but it does show the love held by Toffee supporters for the man who played and managed in their two greatest spells. As part of the Holy Trinity that swept Everton to glory under Harry Catterick in the late Sixties, Kendall has often been dubbed the best player never to be capped by England.

His second coming as manager at Goodison Park did not start well, until two cup runs built the excitement in the blue half of Liverpool, resulting in the FA Cup. It was just the start, as Everton dominated the following season, comfortably beating Liverpool to the title and then following it up with the European Cup Winners' Cup, which remains the last time an English manager has won European silverware. An extra time loss to Manchester United in the FA Cup robbed Kendall of a famous treble.

The mid-Eighties witnessed a titanic struggle between Everton and Liverpool with the league and cups being fought out between them. Everton won the league once more in 1987 and may have tasted more European success if English clubs had not been ostracised following the Heysel disaster. Kendall has since attempted to reach the heights again with various clubs, including returns to Everton, but the golden touch has deserted him.

Howard Kendall (1946–)
Nationality: English.
Managerial honours:
Two English League
Championships, one FA Cup,
one European Cup Winners'
Cup (with Everton).

JACK 'BIG JACK' CHARLTON

> "We also introduced a new word to the players – curfew. Some of them wanted to know if it meant a flightless, long-beaked bird, but they got the message soon enough." Jackie Charlton

Jack Charlton (1935–)
Nationality: English.
Managerial honours:
One Second Division Championship (with Middlesbrough).
Managed Republic of Ireland.

'Big Jack' Charlton, yet another from mining stock, was the Geordie who played for Leeds United, won the World Cup and then became an Irishman. A true 'one club man', he played nearly 800 times at the back for Leeds United, winning silverware as an immovable object during the Don Revie era. His partnership with Bobby Moore in defence for England was instrumental in lifting the nation's sole World Cup, alongside his brother. The image of this great English oak sunk to his knees and weeping into his hands with joy endures to this day.

Despite a successful spell at Middlesbrough, Big Jack will forever be remembered for what he achieved at international level. During his tenure of the Republic of Ireland's team in the late Eighties and early Nineties, they reached three major championships and performed well beyond expectation. Highlights included a famous win over the English in Euro 88, progression to the quarter-finals in Italia 90 and defeating Italy in USA 94 in the sweltering heat, with Jack in his baseball cap looking the archetypal Englishman abroad.

There were disappointments too, especially the last minute goal by eventual winners Holland in 1988, which robbed Ireland of a semi-final place. Indeed, Jack's men succumbed to the Dutch on several important occasions during his reign. He was also fond of giving officials an earful if they crossed him in the heat of battle. But he was a hero of the Irish people, who made him an honorary citizen and gave him the freedom of the city of Dublin. He can't have bought a drink in Ireland since.

JOCK STEIN

"The best place to defend is in the other team's penalty box."

Jock Stein

Of the great Scottish managers – Busby, Shankly, Ferguson – Jock Stein is still thought by many to be the greatest of them all. A stout man with swept back hair as black as the coal he dug as a young man, Stein turned around Celtic fortunes in Glasgow and then took his local side on a famous charge through Europe. While many managers are fortunate to inherit stellar players or a wealthy chairman, Big Jock created a squad from players all born within 30 miles of Celtic Park, moulding them into one of the most aesthetic attacking units the game has witnessed.

Brought up a Rangers fan, the young Stein fell out with his father when he signed for arch rivals Celtic, who he would captain to the 1953 Coronation Cup, beating the cream of British club football. The team won the double the following year, with Stein playing an important role despite continuing his daytime job as a Lanarkshire coal miner. This strong will to overcome odds would serve him well as a manager and with Dunfermline, he quickly made a name for himself, winning the Scottish Cup against his previous employers.

By the time he had turned round Hibernian, Celtic were suffering from one of their worst run of bad results in their history. Stein, the Old Firm club's first non-Catholic manager, immediately shook the club by the scruff of the neck, using both his good-nature and fearful temper to charm and scare the squad into submission. It worked, as the club scooped nine league titles in as many years, as well as numerous doubles and trebles.

Jock Stein (1922–1985)
Nationality: Scottish.
Managerial honours:
One Scottish Cup (with Dunfermline); one Summer Cup (with Hibernian); ten Scottish League Championships, eight Scottish Cups, six League Cups, one European Cup (with Celtic). Managed Scotland.

But it was a balmy evening in Lisbon on 25 May 1967 that granted Stein his finest moment. His Scots were written off against the all-conquering Inter Milan, which had already won two European Cups under mind-games expert Helenio Herrera. Inter, who played a cynical defensive format based on the unpopular *catenaccio* philosophy, took an early lead and then sat back to try and kill off the game. Playing like 'the Dutch speeded up', in reference to the total football of Johan Cruyff and friends, the Lisbon Lions terrorised the Italians with wave after wave of sniping attacks. In the end, the 2-1 scoreline was flattering. When Stein returned home a hero, Shankly wrote to congratulate him with the words, "Jock, you're immortal now."

Many Celtic fans are still piqued that Big Jock never received a knighthood, while Busby and Ferguson did for lifting the European Cup. (Paisley was overlooked too.) But he gained a legacy that few have matched. After leaving Celtic, he enjoyed success with Scotland and it was during a match against Wales in 1985 that Stein died whilst engaged in his greatest passion. His final decision was to substitute Gordon Strachan for Davie Cooper, who scored a penalty to take Scotland through into the World Cup. Minutes later, with the crowd still cheering, Stein was dead.

"I don't believe everything Bill [Shankly] tells me about his players. Had they been that good, they'd not only have won the European Cup but the Ryder Cup, the Boat Race and even the Grand National!" Jock Stein

STAN CULLIS 'IRON MANAGER'

> "Our supporters get more entertainment from watching Wolves than any other two teams put together." Stan Cullis

Stan Cullis regularly appears in lists for the most influential and successful British managers... ever. His Wolverhampton Wanderers were dominant in the late 40s and throughout the 50s, which remains the most successful period in the club's history. Cullis was an inspiration beyond his years, captaining the club at 19, his country at 22 and then becoming the youngest manager to lift the FA Cup at 32 in 1948. As a gaffer, the 'Master of Molineux' kept his squad at the forefront of English club competition for the next decade.

A pioneer of floodlit pitches, the 'Iron Manager' was able to attract international club sides to Molineux to play high profile friendlies, including the Hungarian Army team Honved, which boasted several of the players that had so humbled Walter Winterbottom's England at Wembley in 1953. Cullis' win the following year over the Mighty Magyars in front of 55,000, with the second half streamed live on TV, went a long way to restoring national pride. Cullis proclaimed his team 'champions of the world' to the great indignation of the continental elite, who reacted by setting up the European Cup.

A sergeant-major style enforcer, Cullis' long ball tactics did not always win him the credit he deserved. As Wolves' period of domination subsided in the 60s, Cullis was ignobly sacked by the board, against the wishes of the fans who adored him. At the time, Matt Busby wrote to him in shock, saying "how could people do such a thing after you've given them your life's blood? What more success can they get than you've given them?" A statue by his beloved Molineux has since guaranteed him the enduring respect he was denied back then.

Stan Cullis (1916–2001)
Nationality: English.
Managerial honours: Three English League Championships, two FA Cups (with Wolverhampton Wanderers).

THERE IS NO
FOR HA

JOSE 'THE SPECIAL ONE' MOURINHO

> **"I don't want him [Johan Cruyff] to teach me how to lose 4-0 in a Champions League final because I don't want to learn that."**
>
> Jose Mourinho

"Please don't call me arrogant, but I'm European champion and I think I'm a special one", were the opening lines to an expectant English media when Jose Mourinho arrived at Chelsea Football Club. For ever more he was known as the 'Special One', but he quickly disappointed the sharpened knives by winning back to back league titles, a total of four national titles in a row, including his brace at Porto. He would never lose a match at home, taking six trophies in England in three years. Moving to Inter Milan, Mourinho maintained his home dominance and immediately scooped the Serie A title as well as the Italian Supercup.

Mourinho is the embodiment of the smooth foreign coach, all suave suits and designer shoes, in sharp contrast to the sheepskin or tracksuit of the British gaffer. His George Clooney grey-hair and unwavering self-confidence taught many a lady that newspapers have a sport section. Despite the fluff and bravado, there was also a certain honour to Jose, as he drew criticism when his team played badly, leaving the players to soak in the glory when they won. Criticism of the 'Special One' at Chelsea was largely based on jealousy: he was the young manager with the golden touch and an obscenely wealthy chairman, who the players and fans adored.

His own playing career never got going and it took several years as an apprentice coach before he hit the big time with Porto. Two league titles and two European trophies, including

Jose Mourinho (1963–)
Nationality: Portuguese.
Managerial honours: Two Portuguese League Championships, one Portuguese Cup, one UEFA Cup, one European Cup (with Porto); two English League Championships, two League Cups, one FA Cup (with Chelsea); one Italian League Championship, one Italian Cup (with Inter Milan).

> "Pressure? There is no pressure. Bird Flu is pressure. No, you laugh, but I am being serious. I am more worried about the swan than I am about football."
>
> Jose Mourinho

the big one, put him on every chairman's wish list and it was the Russian billionaire Roman Abramovich who gave the best offer. However, Jose's CV contains the odd controversy, as his passion caused him to lose his usual poise. Although a great fan of Liverpool, he found himself embroiled in various spats with Reds' coach Rafa Benitez, including an accusation of taunting fans during a League Cup final. He was banished from the dug-out although no more action was taken. Subsequent eliminations from the European Cup by Liverpool were greeted with satisfied grunts on Merseyside.

There were also clashes with Arsene Wenger, who he accused of being a 'voyeur', while Jose was fined for his perceived role in the 'tapping up' of Ashley Cole, prior to his transfer from Arsenal. An insinuation that Swedish referee Anders Frisk had been influenced by Barcelona coach Frank Rijkaard in a European Cup tie, led to Frisk retiring amid death threats from fans. Mourinho was again sent to the stands. Finally, Mourinho was cautioned by police after obstructing their plans to quarantine his dog Gullit. Jose is thought to have set the fugitive dog loose through the back door, as officers waited at the front.

In short, it was never dull with Mourinho in the limelight and even opposition managers were disappointed when he parted company with Chelsea. In Italy, he has been quick to court controversy, insulting rival coaches and sports journalists in equal measure. The Portuguese has designs of returning to England in the future, perhaps with Manchester United if the opportunity arises. He would get a warm welcome.

KENNY 'KING KENNY'
DALGLISH

"I was putting myself under enormous pressure to be successful." Kenny Dalglish

'King Kenny' Dalglish was arguably the greatest player to play for Celtic, Liverpool or Scotland. His ability to score great goals in big matches set him apart from even the most brilliant of his team-mates in clubs that dominated their domestic leagues. His exploits on the international stage proved his pedigree further, including goals against the best in the European Cup, as well as famous goals for Scotland such as the winner in the 1977 Wembley pitch invasion and a goal in the world cup win over Holland the next year.

As a manager, first with Liverpool and then Blackburn, the good times still rolled, becoming one of just four gaffers to win the English top flight with more than one club. In charge of Newcastle United in 1997, 'Mystic Kenny' looked set to surpass Tom Watson, Herbert Chapman and Brian Clough to record a third championship winning side, but lost out to Manchester United. A fairytale return to Celtic at the start of the century quickly turned into a nightmare as the league title eluded him.

During his career he witnessed three stadium disasters, which all led to the deaths of fans – experiences that may have contributed to his periods of self-isolation. Following the Hillsborough Tragedy in 1989, he won great admiration for his sympathetic leadership of the club during a harrowing time. But his shyness and dry wit were also interpreted as aloofness, while he has been accused of buckling under pressure. Yet, whenever a big club needs a new manager, Dalglish's name is never far from the top of the list.

Kenny Dalglish (1951–)
Nationality: Scottish.
Managerial honours: Three English League Championships, two FA Cups (with Liverpool); one English League Championship (with Blackburn Rovers); one Scottish League Cup (with Celtic); English League Championship runners-up (with Newcastle United).

KEVIN 'KING KEV'
KEEGAN

"In some ways, cramp is worse than having a broken leg." Kevin Keegan

With a luxuriant mop of hair, tight shorts and tighter trousers, Keegan was the ultimate Seventies footballing pin-up. His playing career was littered with moments of glory with Liverpool, Hamburg and England. However, his trademark passion did get the better of him, most famously during the 1976 Charity Shield match against Leeds, when Keegan was red carded for brawling. Kev removed his shirt and stalked off to the delight of paparazzi and lady spectators alike. The Mighty Mouse's perm duly fronted an advert campaign for Brut aftershave, before singing his own pop song 'Head Over Heels in Love', a top 10 hit (in Germany).

On his second coming at Newcastle as manager at the start of the Nineties, 'King Kev' worked miracles, taking the Geordies back up to the top flight and then to the brink of the biggest prize of all. With teams brimming with attacking flair, his reign coincided with some of the best matches seen in the Premiership, as he tried to score one more goal than the opposition, no matter how many his defence leaked. In 1995, with a 10 point advantage in January, it looked as if Newcastle would win their first league title since Frank Watt's team in 1927. But there was a tragic inevitability to the way Sir Alex Ferguson's Man United reeled them in, as the pressure told on Keegan. His famous rant at Fergie was the beginning of the end for his Geordie dream. "I will love it if we beat them, love it," he railed, finger jabbing at the camera.

Stints with England and then Manchester City followed, but the pressure would grow too much. He tried once more with Newcastle, leading the Toon Army away from relegation, but ultimately the old magic eluded him. However, only a fool would write off a fourth coming in the future!

Kevin Keegan (1951–)
Nationality: English.
Managerial honours: English League Championship runners-up (with Newcastle). Managed England.

STEVE McCLAREN

"I don't read the papers, I don't gamble, I don't even know what day it is!" Steve McClaren

Despite successful coaching stints with Manchester United (he won the treble as assistant coach to Ferguson) and Middlesbrough; it is likely as England manager that Steve McClaren will be forever judged. With a wealth of talent at his disposal, in one of the easiest qualifying groups for Euro 2008, McClaren's outfit spent the summer on the beach. Following the colourful demise of Sven and the snub by Phil Scolari, the FA was honour bound to pick from their own vegetable patch. McClaren, already a coach with the national side, seemed the best of a ropey bunch. But with the charisma of an empty cereal box, Steve's only path to popularity was by winning matches and qualifying for tournaments.

Scolari had cited media pressures as his reason for refusing the job and the Brazilian's concerns soon became the Englishman's reality as the Fleet Street jackals sunk their teeth into any exposed flesh. The manager circled the wagons with corporate jargon, saying that all would be alright in the end; but the poor results and performances soon made the unthinkable a distinct possibility. A limp win over minnows Andorra proved a tipping point, as the supporters roundly booed the team at half-time. "Gentlemen, if you want to write whatever you want to write, you can write it because that is all I am going to say," he said afterwards to the press. The sour relationship had curdled.

Yes, Steve was unlucky with injuries and the highly-paid players have to take some of the blame, especially in the final loss against Croatia. But would other coaches have allowed such apathy on the pitch? When he was finally hounded out, his pockets weighed down with £2.5 million compensation, there were few tears spilt by the players or fans. He is now enjoying success with FC Twente in Holland.

Steve McClaren (1961–)
Nationality: English.
Managerial honours:
One League Cup, UEFA Cup runners-up (with Middlesbrough).
Managed England

MARIO 'THE WOLF' ZAGALLO

> ## "I accept criticism, but what hurts is mockery." Mario Zagallo

When it comes to the World Cup, no individual has enjoyed so much success as Mario Zagallo. A busy left wing, known as *formiguinha* (the little ant), with precise technique and boundless energy to track back in defence, the diminutive Zagallo played alongside Pele and Garrincha for Brazil throughout the World Cup winning campaigns of 1958 and 1962.

Within a decade of winning his second World Cup, Zagallo was back at the finals, but this time as manager. With the talent of players such as Pele, Tostao, Jairzinho, Gerson and Rivelino at his disposal, it ought to have been a struggle not to win the 1970 World Cup. But several star-studded squads have failed to gel in the past, so Zagallo deserves some praise for getting them to play as a team. However, Pele later claimed that Zagallo had attempted to regulate their attacking flair by imposing a rigid formation that moved the players about like chess pieces. The team rebelled and went on to play some of the most attractive football on record.

Zagallo was back in his Mafioso-style big glasses and tracksuit as deputy to Carlos Alberta Perreira at the World Cup in the USA in 1994. Perreira was another coach who believed Brazil needed to dampen their ambition by adhering to white board strategies rather than natural instinct. With stars such as Romario, Bebeto, Leonardo and Branco waiting to be unleashed, the management insisted on a conservative style, which did prevail, albeit on penalties against Italy in the final. Four years later, with Ronaldo suffering on the eve of the Paris final, it was a step too far.

Mario Zagallo (1931–)
Nationality: Brazilian.
Managerial honours:
Two time World Cup winner and one time World Cup runner up (with Brazil).

SIR MATT BUSBY

"It's time to make way for a younger man... a track-suited manager." Sir Matt Busby

Sir Matt Busby was part of the very fabric of Manchester United for almost three decades after the war, building three separate teams to bring a success that only Sir Alex Ferguson has matched. Another ex-miner, the Scotsman's warmth and energy earned him the adoration of players and fans alike, while his remarkable recovery from the serious injuries he received in Munich Air Tragedy of 1958 meant he would be taken to the public's heart.

But for a contractual dispute, Busby could have been a Liverpool man. However, he wanted a club to himself and the opportunity arose at Old Trafford, which was not the force then as it is now. By the time Busby left, however, its legacy as one of the biggest clubs in the world was assured.

His first task was to pick up the pieces after the War. The stadium had been bombed by the Germans, destroying the main stand, dressing rooms and offices, and Busby played his part in the reconstruction process. Busby had served during the War and his leadership qualities shone through as he set about dragging the club back into shape. His keen eye for talent developed a potent attacking force, but perhaps his best signing at that time was right hand man Jimmy Murphy, who would stay with him throughout. This new squad blazed a trail to Wembley in 1948 to win the FA Cup, the first silverware for almost 40 years, and came close on six occasions to winning the league. The spectators poured through the turnstiles, filling the coffers that would pay for the stadium's

Sir Matt Busby (1909–1994)
Nationality: Scottish.
Managerial honours:
Five English League Championships, two FA Cups, one European Cup (with Manchester United).

"If you don't put them in, then you can't know what you've got!" Sir Matt Busby

rebuilding. Busby was not the last canny Scot to recognise the financial benefits of attractive football.

When that team broke up at the start of the 50s, Busby started from scratch with the youth side, famously saying, "if they're good enough, they're old enough." Of course, we will never know how far the Busby Babes would have gone before their fateful return on Flight 609, but the three league championships were surely the start of a glorious era, while youngsters such as Duncan Edwards were tipped for greatness. Busby suffered serious injuries himself, but recovered to lead the club's rehabilitation.

Manchester United might have been excused a period of decline, but Busby was determined to open a new chapter and his steely determination was instrumental in combining the talent that survived the crash with inspirational signings who would sweep the Red Devils to domestic and European Cup glory. Busby released the genius of George Best to create the sport's first pop-style superstar, while Denis Law and Bobby Charlton gelled to form an unrivalled goal-scoring threat. Within just a decade of the crash, Man United won the European Cup in memory of the Busby Babes.

RAFA BENITEZ

> "I can say Liverpool is a joy. My office here is 20 metres long and eight metres wide, it is bigger than the oval office in the White House." Rafa Benitez

You wouldn't have thought that a manager who had guided his team to Champions League triumph and three European semi-finals in three seasons would have to concern themselves with thoughts of the sack, but if the team you manage is Liverpool it would appear that nothing but the League title will do. Despite pressure from fans and the board alike, Rafa Benitez has clung on to his position at the elite club, confident in his ability to bring back the glory days.

Three years at Valencia thrust the neat, groomed thinker into the limelight with two league wins and a UEFA Cup, wresting the stranglehold of Spanish football away from Real Madrid and Barcelona, much as Sir Alex Ferguson had done Aberdeen in the 1970s and 80s. When the board would not meet his transfer requests – "I asked for a table and they bought me a lampshade" – he left for Merseyside. A European Cup in his first season with Liverpool, won in a *Roy of the Rovers* style come-back against AC Milan in Istanbul, hinted that the Rafalution would sweep aside Manchester United, Arsenal and Chelsea to put Liverpool back on top of the league.

It has thus far proved another false dawn at Anfield. An FA Cup and a European Cup runners-up medal have been the only pickings since that famous night and with the Kop (and various owners) baying for the League title, patience is wearing thin. The likeable Spaniard is certainly a Kop favourite but whether he will be given the time to meet the standards of Shankly, Fagan and Paisley remains to be seen.

Rafa Benitez (1960–)
Nationality: Spanish.
Managerial honours:
Two Spanish League Championships, one UEFA Cup (with Valencia); one European Cup, one European Super Cup, one FA Cup (with Liverpool).

RON 'BIG RON' ATKINSON

> ## "There's nobody fitter at his age – except maybe Raquel Welch."
> Ron Atkinson

Ron Atkinson (1939–)
Nationality: English.
Managerial honours:
Two FA Cups (with Manchester United); one League Cup (with Sheffield Wednesday); one League Cup (with Aston Villa).

Orange tan, chunky bling, dark shades and trenchcoat, 'Big Ron' Atkinson was a taste explosion throughout the 1980s and 1990s. An inspirational manager in his time who could unite a squad to excel, Ron is now perhaps more famous for his colourful interpretation of the English language and a racist slur that will hound him for the rest of his media career.

Big Ron really was a half decent manager before he became a TV celebrity. He tasted success at Kettering Town, Cambridge United and West Bromwich Albion. During the mid-80s, Atkinson's Manchester United were consistently near the top of the league, scooping two FA Cups. There were cups too with Sheffield Wednesday and Aston Villa, and various salvage jobs on struggling clubs. It fell away at the end of the century with Nottingham Forest, who bombed despite his hands-on approach. Famously, he climbed into the opposition dug-out before a match, leaving fans wondering whether he was really on their side. A quip that he had provided them with a 'nine goal thriller', having been hammered 8-1 by Man United, enraged the fans further.

All the while, Ron was building up his reputation as a TV pundit, commentating on matches with ITV, alongside Clive Tyldesley. Their partnership proved popular, as Atkinson indulged in his quest to subvert the English language to 'Ronglish.' Some of his phrases and rhyming slang have

"Despite his white boots, he has real pace and aggression."

Ron Atkinson

since passed into the footballer's dictionary, such as early doors (early on in the game), lollipop (step-overs), full gun (a powerful shot) and little eyebrows (a glancing header). Put them all together and you might have something along the lines of, "I tell you what, Clive, that Ronaldo's done a dozen lollipops early doors, crossed the ball to Giggsy, it's gone little eyebrows across the box and Rooney's given it full gun into the back of the net!"

Looking like a spare Don in a *Godfather* movie, Big Ron was always a bit of harmless fun and he was another manager who also enjoyed the sound of his own singing voice, appearing in *Stars in their Eyes* as Frank Sinatra. However, it all turned nasty when he racially insulted black footballer Marcel Desailly believing the microphone was turned off. It wasn't and thousands of listeners across the Middle East heard Ron's outburst. ITV duly turned their back on him, as did his other media contractors, and Ron found himself fighting for his career, telling anyone who would listen that he was not racist. With some justification, he pointed to his early days with West Bromwich Albion, where he had been one of the first managers in the league to sign black players. However, subsequent claims that he was being unfairly hung out to dry did little to help his cause, although he has since returned to broadcasting.

RON GREENWOOD

"Football is a simple game. The hard part is making it look simple." Ron Greenwood

The image of Ron Greenwood with retro-tracksuit and comb-over grey hair at the 1982 World Cup in Spain, when his England were knocked-out despite not losing a game, does not tell the full story. His best work for the national side came in the 1960s, when as manager of West Ham United he played a vital role in developing the trio of Bobby Moore, Geoff Hurst and Martin Peters, who starred in England's 1966 success. Indeed, it was Greenwood who had changed Hurst from an ineffective midfielder to a feared striker, culminating in that hat-trick in the World Cup final.

Greenwood was not a great speech maker nor 'one of the lads' in the dressing room. He had the respect of the players, but could appear aloof and cold. Moore once recalled that in all the years he played under him, he never once said 'well done.' He was not fearful of bringing his players down a peg either, even Moore, who, following a pre-match drinking session, Greenwood stripped of the captaincy and threatened to place on the transfer list, had the club's board not intervened.

Despite his austere exterior, Greenwood was a disciple of open, attacking football, which remains a tenet of West Ham. But by the mid-Seventies, Greenwood had become disillusioned with the modern game. "Other clubs will suffer from the old bugbear that results count more than anything. This has been the ruination of English soccer."

But as England manager, he ultimately turned his back on his own ideals, taking a conservative approach in the World Cup in 1982. His decision to drop Glenn Hoddle after a brilliant debut also caused consternation, which Greenwood shrugged off with the eternal truth that, "disappointment is part of football."

Ron Greenwood (1921–2006) **Nationality:** English. **Managerial honours:** Two FA Cups, one European Cup Winners' Cup (with West Ham United). Managed England.

JOSEF 'SEPP' HERBERGER

> ## "The ball is round, the game lasts 90 minutes, everything else is pure theory." Josef Herberger

Politics and sport should never mix, but that was impossible for any German whose career spanned two World Wars and two national rehabilitations. Indeed, Sepp Herberger's life reflected the peaks and troughs of German football between 1914 and 1954. Like so many other successful managers, Herberger knew what it was to graft outside football, taking his first factory job at the age of 14, before serving in the trenches during the Great War.

As a manager, Herberger was handed the role of national coach in 1936 at the peak of Hitler's powers. With the Fuhrer breathing down its neck, the team went unbeaten in 1937, although the opposition were often handpicked to be a walkover. The bubble burst in 1938, as Germany were thumped 3-6 at home by England (who famously gave the raised-arm salute), before bombing in the World Cup that year. Although there is little evidence that he was an member of the Nazi party, it is widely accepted that Herberger did little to stop football being used as a pawn in the propaganda machine. Indeed, he helped produce a propaganda film in 1941 titled, 'The Great Game.'

However, Herberger's first love was for the national team and he was instrumental in rebuilding it after the war. The first match in 1950 against Switzerland was watched by 115,000 spectators and his football team became the inspiration for Germany's remarkable rehabilitation in a way that it never was for the Nazi Party. The climax came in the 1954 World Cup final when desire, guts and a rain storm drove the team to glory in the 'Miracle of Berne', beating the Mighty Magyars of Hungary against all odds. German football has rarely looked back.

Josef Herberger
(1897–1977)
Nationality: German.
Managerial honours: One World Cup (with West Germany).

TERRY 'EL TEL' VENABLES

> "I had mixed feelings – like watching your mother-in-law drive over a cliff in your car."
>
> Terry Venables

Terry Venables is a charming wheeler-dealer who can talk his way in and out of trouble. With a reputation for tactical astuteness and an ability to relate to players in the changing room, Venables has all the attributes for success on the biggest stage. However, being a favourite of the tabloid press has not always sat well with prospective employers.

'El Tel' bridged the language gap with mighty Barcelona to win La Liga, also reaching the final of the European Cup. He then returned to White Hart Lane where he fell in and out with Sir Alan Sugar, resulting in a High Court trial, which he had to pay for. It was not the last time he would be stung for his dodgy dealings. But by 1993, Graham Taylor had made a mess of his England aspirations and the FA decided Venables was the man to lead the nation at home in Euro 96.

It was a happy time for Tel, who got the best out of players such as Alan Shearer, Teddy Sheringham and Paul Gascoigne, culminating in a rampant 4-1 defeat of Holland, as the country thought "football was coming home". Of course, that song is now a lasting hit in Germany, who burst England's bubble on penalties in the semi-finals.

Since then, he has struggled to hit the dizzy heights again. His non-football affairs have continued, however, including several novels, a detective TV drama, media punditry and the pop song England Crazy with Rider in 2002 which reached number 46 in the UK charts.

Terry Venables (1943–)
Nationality: English.
Managerial honours: One English Second Division Championship, FA Cup runners-up (with Queens Park Rangers); European Cup runners-up, Spanish League Championship, one Spanish League Cup (with Barcelona); one FA Cup (with Tottenham Hotspur). Managed England and Australia.

TOMMY DOCHERTY

'THE DOC'

> "Players today are a pack of overpaid, pampered, snot nose little ponces. Bring back National Service for the lot of the bastards."
>
> Tommy Docherty

Controversy followed Tommy Docherty throughout his playing and management career, but he has made a good living from the game and provided entertainment for fans, players and journalists alike. While the numerous club chairmen who dispensed with his services may not agree, 'the Doc' remains one of the most colourful characters to have roamed the dug out.

A natural talker and motivator, he quickly took to management and led Chelsea back to the top flight, creating a successful team of youngsters, including Terry Venables, called the 'Docherty Diamonds' in the mid-60s. His reputation built, Docherty set about dismantling it, riding a roller-coaster of different clubs, including Manchester United, QPR, Derby County, Oporto, Wolves, Aston Villa, Preston North End, Hull, Scotland and a couple more in Australia. "I've had more clubs than Jack Nicklaus," is one of his many one-liners.

There were good times with Manchester United, as he guided the Red Devils back to the First Division and then took them to Wembley in consecutive years. However, just months after an FA Cup win, he was dismissed for having an affair with the wife of the club's physiotherapist. The club appeared to have let him off, but then pressure from the players' wives proved too strong and he was sacked. Within days of his dismissal, he appeared in public sporting a black eye dealt out by the jilted husband.

Tommy Docherty (1928–)
Nationality: Scottish.
Managerial honours:
One League Cup (with Chelsea); one FA Cup (with Manchester United). Managed Scotland.

SIR WALTER WINTERBOTTOM

> "There cannot be many men in the game who see the theory, practice and politics of football as clearly as Walter does."
>
> Bobby Charlton

Sir Walter Winterbottom was a great servant of the English game, who is credited for modernising coaching and setting the benchmark for domestic managers to follow. He was England's longest serving manager, overseeing 139 matches and winning 78 of them. Taking up the reins after the Second World War, his team helped to bring a smile back to the nation, competing well in the Home Nations' championships, which were a priority in those days. However, Winterbottom's task was made trickier by the fact he did not have complete control of team selection, limiting his role to that of an administrator rather than outright gaffer.

Nonetheless, he had a direct influence on the way his team played, improving such luminaries as Tom Finney and Stanley Matthews. But his era is devoid of World Cup success, failing to pass the quarter-finals in four attempts. There were also the high profile defeat to lowly USA in Brazil 1950 and the two hammerings by the Mighty Magyars in 1953/4 that highlighted England's frailties. Winterbottom was a lone voice at the time, saying that the Hungarians should not be taken lightly. "The press tended to think we would win easily but I tried to point out that the Hungarians were actually a great side."

Nowadays, 16 years as English manager could never pass with so little incident!

Sir Walter Winterbottom
(1913–2002)
Nationality: English.
Managerial honours:
Managed England.

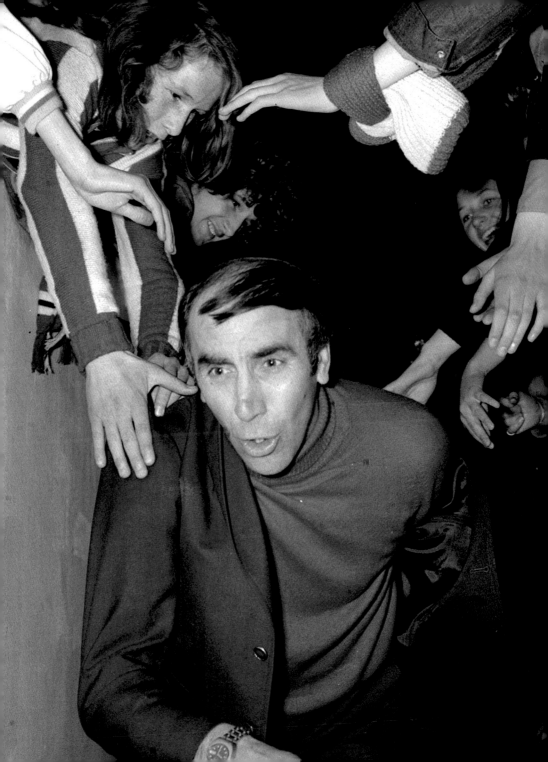

BOB STOKOE

> "I didn't bring the magic. It was always here. I just came back to find it." Bob Stokoe

If you wanted one moment to embody the magic of the FA Cup, then a good starting point is Sunderland's Bob Stokoe sprinting across the Wembley turf in 1973 to engulf his triumphant goalkeeper Jimmy Montgomery for defying mighty Leeds United. Porkpie hat and beige raincoat flowing above his red tracksuit, with a grin as wide as the Wearmouth Bridge, Stokoe was living the dream of every journeyman manager.

The victory was made even sweeter given Stokoe's bitter feud with Leeds' supremo Don Revie, who the usually courteous Geordie accused of attempting to bribe his Bury team 11 years earlier. "Revie was always an evil man to me," he later said. In the run up to the match, Stokoe delighted the media by baiting Revie, including a cheap jibe at his 'lucky suit'. It was like David taunting Goliath about his loin cloth before their fight.

In front of 100,000 spectators, using an orange ball, the Mackems took a first half lead. Leeds replied with wave upon wave of attacks, only to be thwarted by Montgomery's heroic efforts, including a double save against Trevor Cherry and Peter Lorimer, which still rank as some of the greatest in the cup's history. The sheet stayed clean and Stokoe set off on his victory dash, watched by a dazed Revie.

Bobby Charlton may be the greatest exponent of the footballing comb-over; but Stokoe deserves an honourable mention. He was also famous for his successful cross-over from rivals Newcastle United, with whom he won the FA Cup as a player, to Sunderland. When he died in 2004, his funeral was packed with supporters from both sets of fans, proof that depth of character is more important than tribal instinct.

Bob Stokoe (1930–2004)
Nationality: English.
Managerial honours:
One Anglo-Italian Cup (with Blackpool); one English second Division Championship; one FA Cup (with Sunderland).

CÉSAR LUIS MENOTTI 'EL FLACO'

> ## "A goal should be just another pass into the net."
> César Luis Menotti

Known throughout his career as 'El Flaco' (the thin man), César Luis Menotti was the non-conformist who gave conformity to the Argentine national team. With his long hair, casual dress sense and left wing views, Menotti was the most unlikely man to win favour with the establishment following General Galtieri's military junta in 1976. But for the first half of his career, at least, the authorities were wise to listen to his demands, as they resulted in stylish teams that won trophies.

Having played out a commendable career, the one-time strike partner of Pele at Santos formed a Huracan outfit that was loaded with attacking tyros who swept all before them to the club's first domestic league title.

Before Menotti, the national coach had a shelf life of fresh milk; but with Argentina set to host the World Cup in 1978, Menotti was given time to build a side that could lift the trophy for the first time in the country's history. But as the circus arrived in '78, the critics were still sharpening their knives, especially when Menotti stubbornly picked the veteran striker Mario Kempes instead of 17-year old wonder kid Diego Maradona. Kempes duly scored two goals in the final against Holland to send the country into raptures. That night, *El Flaco* put on a disguise and joined in the street party.

The following year, Maradona announced his arrival on the world stage as part of a team that played sublime football in winning the World Youth Cup in Japan. It was Menotti who helped release such a prodigious talent. Indeed, to this day, Argentineans who believe that style and flair is a better mindset for football, rather than 'results at any cost', still call themselves *Menottistas*.

César Luis Menotti (1927–)
Nationality: Argentina
Managerial honours: one World Cup, one World Youth Cup (with Argentina); one Argentine League Championship (with Huracan); one Spanish Cup, one League Cup (with Barcelona).

ENZO BEARZOT

> "Football is first and foremost a game." Enzo Bearzot

The entertainer with the smoking pipe and easy smile remains the most beloved of Italian coaches in his native country following the sweep to glory during the 1982 World Cup in Spain. Bearzot had already managed the team for the best part of a decade beforehand, instilling a flamboyant style and building a squad that could call on two expert technicians in each position. But as with several teams to lift the Cup, Italy were late starters in 1982, scraping through the qualifiers and peaking at the end of the tournament. Following widespread press criticism, Bearzot famously announced a media blackout, which would be unthinkable nowadays, and hid his team away to build unity. As with manager Marcello Lippi in 2006, these close confines allowed Bearzot to impart his considerable charisma and the *Azzurri* re-emerged a changed force.

At the forefront was goal sensation Paolo Rossi, who had just finished a long suspension over match-fixing allegations, who Bearzot insisted on picking despite scathing attacks in the national papers. But, having dispatched the defending champions Argentina, Rossi scored a hat-trick against the star-studded Brazilians in the quarters; a brace against Poland; and then the opener against West Germany in the final. Bearzot had stayed loyal to his main man, who he knew was their best chance of success. On the final whistle, the squad lifted Bearzot on their shoulders, as a tribute to the role he had played.

Enzo Bearzot (1927–)
Nationality: Italian.
Managerial honours:
One World Cup (with Italy).

GORDON STRACHAN

"I tried to get the disappointment out of my system by going for a walk. I ended up 17 miles from home..." Gordon Strachan

Gordon Strachan was a pint-sized scrapper who punched well above his weight as a player and he is proving to be every bit as combative as a manager. Part of the winning Aberdeen team under Alex Ferguson, Strachan also played a leading role in Leeds United's surge to the English title under Howard Wilkinson in 1992, the last time that an English manager has won that crown.

As a manager, first of Coventry and then Southampton, Strachan achieved several Houdini-style escapes from relegation, before temporarily calling it a day on personal grounds. The dug-out's loss was the TV studio's gain, as viewers warmed to Strachan's deadpan humour and deep understanding of the game during punditry on the BBC's *Match of the Day*. His observations have made it into folklore, such as this gem about Wayne Rooney. "It's an incredible rise to stardom. At 17 you're more likely to get a call from Michael Jackson than Sven-Goran Eriksson."

Celtic coaxed him back into coaching and he soon began amassing silverware. The Bhoys claimed impressive scalps in Europe and went further in the Champions League than any Scottish club before. Three league titles were clinched in a row, but he resigned in 2009. He has since signed on as coach of Middlesbrough. As a player he put his longevity down to a good diet, an experience he hands onto his own charges, including supplements such as seaweed. Perhaps that is Strachan's endearing trait: he gives the impression there is much more to his life than football. One hack once asked him, "and the main is thing is to win tomorrow?" To which Strachan replied, "No, no. The main thing is to enjoy life and all the rest of it, and be healthy."

Gordon Strachan (1957–)
Nationality: Scottish.
Managerial honours:
FA Cup runners-up (with Southampton); three Scottish League Championships, two Scottish Cup, two Scottish League Cup (with Celtic).

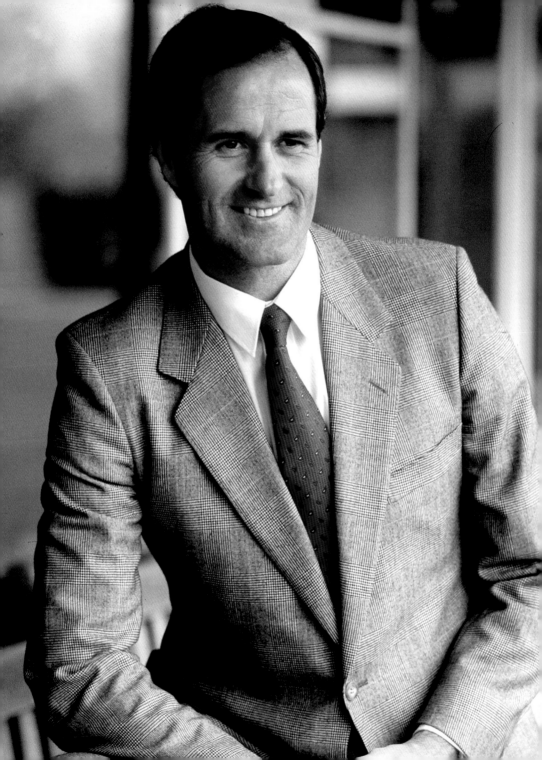

GEORGE GRAHAM

> ## "They haven't lived up to the expectations we expect of them." George Graham

There are managers who court popularity with their manner and footballing style, while others believe that results are all that matter. George Graham is a champion of the second category. Indeed, it seemed to be a personal challenge to put the wind up as many critics as possible.

"Hello, George, it's nice to have you back," said his secretary, when the ex-player first arrived at Highbury as manager. "It's Mister Graham now," came the short reply. Mister Graham was determined to instil a new ethos at the north London club, which had struggled for over a decade and he did so by clearing out the old dead wood and building a squad based on young talent. They bought into his mindset and the trophies began to rack up, including the coveted league title twice. However, as the reign continued, so the style became ever more conservative, with the team dominated by its 'flat back four' and chants of '1-0 to the Arsenal'. Graham delighted in the criticism, stating, "yes, winning is boring, isn't it?"

But the wind fell from his sails when accusations of taking bungs during player transfers led to his dismissal, prompting Graham to accuse the club of holding a kangaroo court. A moderate spell at Leeds preceded a shock move to Arsenal's great enemies Tottenham Hotspur, whose free-flowing tradition seemed to grate against Graham's lack of flair. Why did he take the job? Possibly because he saw an opportunity to take a proud old club back to the big time. More likely it was a case of sheer bloody-mindedness.

George Graham (1944–)
Nationality: Scottish.
Managerial honours:
Two English League Championships, two League Cups, one FA Cup, one European Cup Winners' Cup (with Arsenal); one League Cup (with Tottenham Hotspur).

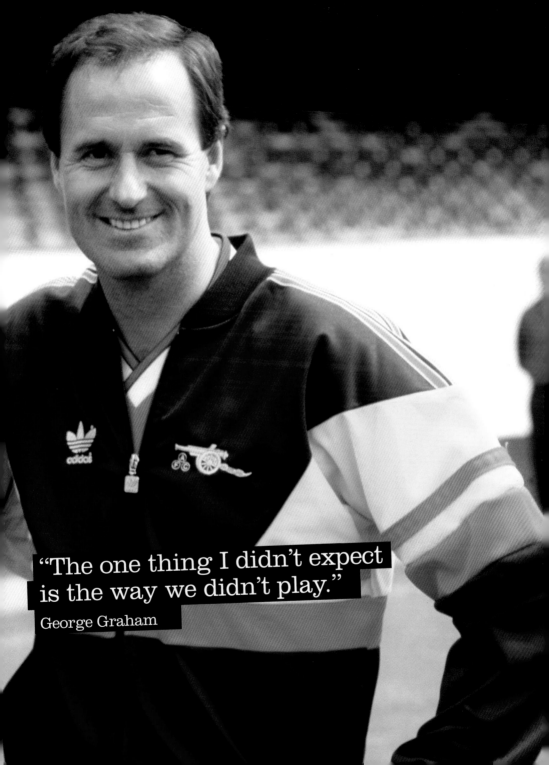

"The one thing I didn't expect is the way we didn't play."

George Graham

NEIL WARNOCK

"Matches don't come any bigger than FA Cup quarter-finals."

Neil Warnock

Neil Warnock is the English manager that so many clubs love to hate. Whether it is opposition players, managers, fans, chairmen or the officials, Warnock will say what first enters his mind, even if it lands him in boiling water. Referred to as Colin by several sets of rival fans on account of its anagram potential, Warnock, the current coach of Queens Park Rangers is also a qualified chiropodist and referee. He is renowned as a play-off specialist, securing promotion at Wembley on five occasions in nine years. He led Sheffield United on cup runs to the semi-finals of both the FA Cup and League Cup in the same year, later taking them to the Premier League.

However, matches rarely passed without incident. He fell out with Liverpool, having accused defender Stephane Henchoz of spitting at him. He fell out with West Brom manager Gary Megson, who claimed Warnock tried to render the match null and void reducing his team to six players. Now called the 'Battle of Bramall Lane', Sheffield had three men sent off. When two went down injured, they could only field six and the match was abandoned with Megson's team 3-0 up. Sheffield were eventually fined £10,000 and the result stood.

Warnock liked to have a pop at referees, calling David Ellery "that bald bloke" and berating Graham Poll. He even fell out with Sheffield fan and A-list movie star Sean Bean, who he accused of swearing in front of his wife and kids. Warnock was also sent to the stands for doing a V-sign at Norwich manager Nigel Worthington, who had refused to shake hands with him.

"I'm determined to enjoy it," he said, when he joined the Premier League. "I won't be quiet, but I won't be the nutcase people expect me to be. There are only 20 managers in the best league in the world, and I'm one of them. It takes some believing."

Neil Warnock (1948–)
Nationality: English.
Managerial honours:
Five English League play-off promotions, FA Cup and League Cup semi-finalist (with Sheffield United).

SIR ALF RAMSEY

> "As a manager, Alf Ramsey is like a good chicken farmer. If a hen doesn't lay, a good chicken farmer wrings its neck." Jackie Milburn

Sir Alf Ramsey remains the most successful manager to lead England on the basis that he snared the World Cup for the lone time in the nation's history. His generous nature made him a favourite with the players and crowd, while his astute tactical mind played as big role in the victory in 1966 as Geoff Hurst, Bobby Moore or the Russian linesman.

Sir Alf was famously captured looking serene and unfazed as England clinched the Jules Rimet trophy. He later commented that he was simply watching the play and calculating his options. This down-to-earth, analytical approach could be interpreted as cold and aloof by his detractors, and he often rubbed up people the wrong way with his brusque and bolshy mannerisms. However, it served him well as a right back during an illustrious career with Spurs and England. Known as 'the General' even then for his sound decision making and ability to read the game, Ramsey made up for a lack of pace with speed of mind. However, it was too slow for the trickery of the Hungarian Mighty Magyars in 1953, the final match of his international playing career.

Having hung up his boots, Ramsey took to management like an Italian to theatre. He quickly led Ipswich Town from the third division to the peak of the league, an accomplishment which made him a legend at Portman Road well before his England days. But when the national team came calling in 1963, he was unable to refuse, announcing

Sir Alf Ramsey (1920–1999)
Nationality: English.
Managerial honours:
One English League Championship (with Ipswich Town); one World Cup (with England).

> ## "The missing of chances is one of the mysteries of life."
> Sir Alf Ramsey

immediately that England would win the World Cup in their home tournament. It was a bold statement given the slim pickings in the past, but it always looks better if you're right.

At the start of the World Cup, it seemed that Ramsey had spoken too soon, following a 0-0 draw with Uruguay, but his tinkering bore fruit as the right formation began to bang in the goals. His resistance to calls for Nobby Stiles to be dropped following a vicious tackle won him support in the camp, while his gamble to play without wingers and then pick Geoff Hurst over fit-again Jimmy Greaves in the final, have been acclaimed as masterful.

The rest of his management career did not hit those dizzy heights. There was the loss to Jim Baxter's Scots in 1967, then the disappointment of being knocked out in the 1970 quarter-finals, when his cautious tactics at 2-0 up to the Germans was partly to blame. Finally, a draw against Poland in 1973 ended qualification hopes for the 1974 World Cup and he was sacked. However, Sir Alf had long since booked his place in English football folklore.

BILL NICHOLSON

> "The public can't be kidded. They know what they want to see, what is good and what is bad and what is just average." Bill Nicholson

In 1936, Bill Nicholson, who was working as a laundry man in his home town of Scarborough, received an offer to join Spurs at the age of 17 for £2 a week. He would be associated with the club for the next 68 years and provide their supporters with the greatest moments in the club's history. Thick set, with a distinctive short-back-and-sides haircut, Nicholson lost most of his playing career to the War, during which he worked as sergeant-instructor, training new recruits, latterly at a camp in Italy inherited from Wolves' supremo Stan Cullis. Not that he was bitter to lose so many years, saying that "what I did for six years in the Army taught me how to handle people and how to talk to people."

After the War, Nicholson's robust midfield play won back his place in front of a young Alf Ramsey, in the famous 'push and run' Spurs team, that gained promotion to the first division and then won the title. 'Mr Tottenham' won just the one cap for England, scoring with his first touch after just 19 seconds, but never played another. Again, he was philosophical, saying his replacement was a better player and that "my duty is to get fit for Tottenham. Well, they pay my wages, don't they?"

When he retired, Spurs were keen to keep hold of his tactical awareness and so promoted him to manager. Within

Bill Nicholson (1919–2004)
Nationality: English.
Managerial honours:
One English League Championship, three FA Cups, two League Cups, one European Cup Winners' Cup, one UEFA Cup (with Tottenham Hotspur).

"If you don't win anything, you have had a bad season."
Bill Nicholson

just two years, his Spurs side had swept all before them, winning a unique double of the league and FA Cup, scoring 115 goals in 42 games. It was the start of good times at White Hart Lane, including two more FA Cups and long forays into Europe, returning with the Cup Winners' Cup, the first European trophy won by an English team. Not that the deadpan manager was much impressed by the win, saying, "We did nothing. We didn't play. We didn't even start to play."

Throughout his long vigil at Spurs, Nicholson maintained a low profile, preferring to let the flowing, attractive style on the pitch do the talking for him. Only once was he dramatically drawn out of his shell, during the 1974 UEFA Cup final loss to Dutch side Feyenoord. As Spurs fans rioted during the away second-leg, injuring several opposition supporters, Nicholson took hold of the public address microphone to ask for calm, saying "you people make me feel ashamed to be an Englishman."

He retired soon afterwards, saying he had fallen out of sync with the style and politics of modern football, but Spurs ensured he remained on the board in a consultancy role. A true one-club man, Mr Tottenham was widely mourned when he died in 2004.

Bob Stokoe

Ron Atkinson

This book would not have been possible without the kind assistance of the following people: Brian Attmore, Stephen Done, Rob Mason, Marie Spence, Jane Whitehead and Sandra E. Dobbs.

"Who'd be a football manager?
I would every time!"
Harry Redknapp

First published in 2008 as *Football Managers:*
The Lives and Half-times by Prion
an imprint of the Carlton Publishng Group
20 Mortimer Street
London W1T 3JW

This revised paperback edition published in 2010 by Prion

10 9 8 7 6 5 4 3 2 1

A CIP catalogue record for this book is available from British Library.

ISBN: 978-1-85375-772-3

Designed by: Pretty-Effective-Design.com
Editorial: John Behan
Picture Research: Paul Langan
Production: Lisa French